U•X•L
American Decades
1970•1979

Rob Nagel, Editor

Detroit • New York • San Diego • San Francisco • Cleveland • New Haven, Conn. • Waterville, Maine • London • Munich

U•X•L American Decades, 1970–1979

Rob Nagel, Editor

Project Editors
Diane Sawinski, Julie L. Carnagie, and Christine Slovey

Editorial
Elizabeth Anderson

Permissions
Shalice Shah-Caldwell

Imaging and Multimedia
Dean Dauphinais

Product Design
Pamela A.E. Galbreath

Composition
Evi Seoud

Manufacturing
Rita Wimberley

For more information, contact:
The Gale Group, Inc.
27500 Drake Rd.
Farmington Hills, MI 48331-3535
Or you can visit our Internet site at
http://www.gale.com

Vol. 1: 0-7876-6455-3
Vol. 2: 0-7876-6456-1
Vol. 3: 0-7876-6457-X
Vol. 4: 0-7876-6458-8
Vol. 5: 0-7876-6459-6
Vol. 6: 0-7876-6460-X
Vol. 7: 0-7876-6461-8
Vol. 8: 0-7876-6462-6
Vol. 9: 0-7876-6463-4
Vol. 10: 0-7876-6464-2

LIBRARY OF CONGRESS CATALOGING-IN-PUBLICATION DATA

U•X•L American decades
p. cm.
Includes bibliographical references and index.
Contents: v. 1. 1900-1910—v. 2. 1910-1919—v. 3.1920-1929—v. 4. 1930-1939—v. 5. 1940-1949—v. 6. 1950-1959—v. 7. 1960-1969—v. 8. 1970-1979—v. 9.1980-1989—v. 10. 1990-1999.
Summary: A ten-volume overview of the twentieth century which explores such topics as the arts, economy, education, government, politics, fashions, health, science, technology, and sports which characterize each decade.
ISBN 0-7876-6454-5 (set: hardcover: alk. paper)
1. United States—Civilization—20th century—Juvenile literature. 2. United States—History—20th century—Juvenile literature. [1. United States—Civilization—20th century. 2. United States—History—20th century.] I. UXL (Firm) II. Title: UXL American decades. III. Title: American decades.
E169.1.U88 2003
973.91—dc21
2002010176

Printed in the United States of America
10 9 8 7 6 5 4 3 2 1

Contents

Reader's Guide

U•X•L American Decades provides a broad overview of the major events and people that helped to shape American society throughout the twentieth century. Each volume in this ten-volume set chronicles a single decade and begins with an introduction to that decade and a timeline of major events in twentieth-century America. Following are eight chapters devoted to these categories of American endeavor:

- Arts and Entertainment
- Business and the Economy
- Education
- Government, Politics, and Law
- Lifestyles and Social Trends
- Medicine and Health
- Science and Technology
- Sports

These chapters are then divided into five sections:

Chronology: A timeline of significant events within the chapter's particular field.

✻ **Overview:** A summary of the events and people detailed in that chapter.

★ **Headline Makers:** Short biographical accounts of key people and their achievements during the decade.

- **Topics in the News:** A series of short topical essays describing events and people within the chapter's theme.
- **For More Information:** A section that lists books and Web sites directing the student to further information about the events and people covered in the chapter.

OTHER FEATURES

Each volume of *U•X•L American Decades* contains more than eighty black-and-white photographs and illustrations that bring the events and people discussed to life and sidebar boxes that expand on items of high interest to readers. Concluding each volume is a general bibliography of books and Web sites that explore the particular decade in general and a thorough subject index that allows readers to easily locate the events, people, and places discussed throughout that volume of *U•X•L American Decades.*

COMMENTS AND SUGGESTIONS

We welcome your comments on *U•X•L American Decades* and suggestions for other history topics to consider. Please write: Editors, *U•X•L American Decades,* U•X•L, 27500 Drake Rd., Farmington Hills, MI 48331-3535; call toll-free: 1-800-877-4253; fax: 248-699-8097; or send e-mail via http://www.galegroup.com.

Chronology of the 1970s

1970: The floppy disk is introduced for storing computer information.

1970: *American Top 40*, a weekly countdown of hits on the pop music charts hosted by Casey Kasem, debuts on nationwide radio.

1970: Police touch off a riot in the barrio of East Los Angeles, resulting in the death of prominent Hispanic journalist Ruben Salazar and inspiring the growing Chicano consciousness movement.

1970: **January 21** The Boeing 747, the first jumbo jet, is put into commercial service.

1970: **February 8** At a Birmingham rally, former Alabama governor George Wallace urges southern governors to defy federal education integration orders.

1970: **February 20** U.S. Secretary of State Henry Kissinger begins secret talks in Paris with Le Duc Tho, representative of North Vietnam, toward ending the Vietnam War.

1970: **March 25** The first major postal workers' strike in American history ends after seven days.

1970: **April 22** The first Earth Day is celebrated.

1970: **May 4** Four students are killed and eight wounded at Kent State University in Ohio by National Guard troops at a student rally protesting the Vietnam War.

1970: **August 12** In a case brought by Philadelphia Phillies outfielder Curt Flood, federal court judge Ben Cooper rules that a 1922 U.S. Supreme Court decision finding that organized baseball does not violate antitrust laws is still binding. The Major League Baseball Players Association announces it will take the case to the U.S. Supreme Court.

1970: **October 26** The federal government mandates the use of unleaded gasoline in federal vehicles.

1970: **December 30** The U.S. Congress passes the Poison Prevention Packaging Act, requiring manufacturers of potentially dangerous products to put safety tops on their containers so children will not be able to open them. The law takes effect in 1972.

1971: Intel introduces the first computer chip (microprocessor).

1971: Texas Instruments introduces the first pocket calculator, weighing 2.5 pounds and costing around $150.

1971: The Twenty-Sixth Amendment to the U.S. Constitution, lowering the voting age from twenty-one to eighteen, is ratified.

1971: **January 1** Cigarette advertising on U.S. radio and television is banned.

1971: **March 8** The U.S. Supreme Court prohibits employers from using job tests that discriminate against African Americans.

1971: **March 29** U.S. Army First Lieutenant William Calley is found guilty of murder in the 1968 massacre of Vietnamese civilians at My Lai.

1971: **April 20** The U.S. Supreme Court unanimously rules that busing to achieve racial balance is constitutional in cases where local officials permitted segregation to occur.

1971: **June 10** President Richard Nixon ends a twenty-year trade embargo against Communist China.

1971: **September 9** Prisoners riot at the Attica State Correctional Facility in Attica, New York. After four days, Governor Nelson Rockefeller orders the state police to retake the prison by force.

1972: The U.S. Congress approves the Equal Rights Amendment (ERA) and sends it to the states to be ratified.

1972: Phyllis Schlafly organizes the National Committee to Stop ERA.

1972: The Dow-Jones average hits 1,000 for the first time in history.

1972: **January 10** The U.S. Surgeon General's report on smoking warns that nonsmokers exposed to cigarette smoke may suffer health risks.

1972: **February 21** President Nixon becomes the first U.S. president to visit Communist China.

1972: **March 22** The *Pioneer 10* space probe is launched to explore the outer planets; on June 13, 1983, it becomes the first human-created object to leave the solar system.

1972: **June 14** Following warnings that DDT is interfering with the reproduction of birds and is potentially toxic to humans, the Environmental Protection Agency (EPA) announces a ban on most uses of pesticides, beginning December 31.

1972: **June 17** Police arrest five men for breaking into the Democratic National Committee's headquarters at the Watergate office complex in Washington, D.C. Three of the men have ties to Richard Nixon's reelection campaign.

1972: **June 19** The U.S. Supreme Court reaffirms the exemption of professional baseball from antitrust laws.

1972: **November 16** PepsiCo announces a deal to sell its products in the Soviet Union.

1973: Three men are elected as the first African American mayors in three major American cities: Maynard Jackson in Atlanta, Thomas Bradley in Los Angeles, and Coleman Young in Detroit.

1973: The American Psychiatric Association removes homosexuality from its list of mental illnesses, redefining it as a "sexual orientation disturbance."

1973: The U.S. Congress passes the HMO Act, regulating Health Maintenance Organizations.

1973: **January 22** The U.S. Supreme Court rules in *Roe* v. *Wade* by a vote of six to three that women's interest in privacy means that states cannot prohibit abortion in the first trimester of pregnancy.

1973: **January 27** In Paris, Henry Kissinger and Le Duc Tho sign the cease-fire agreement on the Vietnam War.

1973: **March** The English rock group Pink Floyd releases its landmark album *The Dark Side of the Moon*. It remains on the *Billboard* Top 200 Albums chart for 741 weeks.

1973: **May 25** The first Skylab mission is launched. A three-man crew conducts experiments for twenty-eight days in this orbiting space station.

1973: **June 25–29** Former White House counsel John Dean testifies before the Ervin committee, implicating himself, H. R. Haldeman, John Ehrlichman, John Mitchell, President Richard Nixon, and others in the Watergate cover-up.

1973: **September 21** Billie Jean King defeats Bobby Riggs in a highly publicized tennis match billed as the Battle of the Sexes.

1973: **October** Following the beginning of the Yom Kippur War between Israel and Arab states, some members of the Organization of Petroleum Exporting Countries (OPEC) begin an embargo of oil to the United States and other Western nations.

1973: **October 23** Eight resolutions to impeach President Nixon are introduced in the U.S. House of Representatives.

1973: **November 13** The U.S. Department of Health, Education, and Welfare rejects college desegregation plans filed by state systems in Arkansas, Florida, Georgia, Louisiana, Mississippi, North Carolina, Oklahoma, Pennsylvania, and Virginia.

1973: **Decenber 22** As a fuel-conservation and safety measure, the U.S. Congress orders states to reduce interstate speed limits to 55 MPH.

1973: **December 26** *The Exorcist,* based on the best-selling novel of the same name by William Peter Blatty, debuts in theaters. The terrifying film initially created mass hysteria, with some viewers fainting in theaters.

1974: Scientists warn that chlorofluorocarbons (CFCs) used as propellents in spray cans may be destroying the ozone layer of Earth's atmosphere.

1974: Disco, a beat-driven dance music already popular in the black and gay communities, begins to find mainstream success behind such hits as "Rock the Boat," "Rock Your Baby," and "Kung Fu Fighting."

1974: **January 17** The U.S. Department of Health, Education, and Welfare says racial discrimination still exists in the schools in Topeka, Kansas, the site of the landmark 1954 educational segregation lawsuit *Brown* v. *Board of Education of Topeka.*

1974: **February 4** In Berkeley, California, nineteen-year-old newspaper heiress Patricia Hearst is kidnapped by the Symbionese Liberation Army.

1974: **April 8** Hank Aaron breaks Babe Ruth's career home run record, hitting number 715.

1974: **June** The Heimlich manuever is introduced as first aid for choking.

1974: **August 8** In a televised address, President Nixon announces his resignation from the presidency, effective at noon on August 9. He becomes the first president in American history to resign.

1974: **September 14** White mobs in Boston greet buses carrying African Americans to their schools by shouting racist remarks. Violence ensues. A month later, Massachusetts governor Francis Sargent calls out the National Guard to restore order in South Boston.

1974: **October 3** Frank Robinson is named manager of the Cleveland Indians, becoming the first African American manager in major league baseball.

1974: **October 8** President Gerald Ford announces his program to control inflation, called Whip Inflation Now (WIN). Despite a denial by President Ford, the chairman of the federal reserve, Arthur Burns, states that a recession is under way.

1975: The first personal computer, the Altair 8800, is introduced in kit form.

1975: The first strike by U.S. doctors is carried out in New York City hospitals.

1975: Lyme disease is identified in Lyme, Connecticut.

1975: Exxon Corporation replaces General Motors as the nation's wealthiest company.

1975: **February 7** The federal government reports January unemployment at 8.2 percent, the highest level since 1941.

1975: **March 27** Construction of the nearly 800-mile Trans-Alaska Pipeline begins.

1975: **April 29** The last Americans leave the U.S. embassy in Saigon. General Duong Van Minh of the South Vietnamese army surrenders to the North Vietnamese the following day.

1975: **July 5** Arthur Ashe defeats Jimmy Connors to win the Wimbledon men's singles championship, becoming the first African American to do so.

1975: **July 15** The American-Soviet *Apollo-Soyuz* orbiting space station is launched.

1975: **August 1** Indianapolis city schools are ordered to transfer 6,533 African American students to eight suburban school districts.

1976: The National Aeronautics and Space Administration (NASA) accepts its first female astronaut trainees.

1976: Karen Ann Quinlan's parents win a court battle to turn off the respirator keeping their comatose daughter alive.

1976: An outbreak of Legionnaires' disease occurs at the Philadelphia convention of the American Legion. Twenty-nine die.

1976: American writer Saul Bellow wins the Nobel Prize for literature.

1976: A swine-flu epidemic threatens the United States. Millions are vaccinated, but the warning turns out to be a false alarm.

1976: **March 26** The federal government accuses the Encyclopaedia Britannica Company of deceptive selling and other practices.

1976: **July 3–4** The nation celebrates the two-hundreth anniversary of its independence with festivals and political events around the country.

1976: **December 18** Over 175 U.S. companies admit bribery in excess of $300 million since 1970.

1977: The Apple II, the first successful personal computer, is introduced.

1977: **January 21** President Jimmy Carter signs an unconditional pardon for almost all Vietnam-era draft evaders.

1977: **February 20** Alex Haley's *Roots* is listed by the *New York Times* as the top-selling book in the country for twenty consecutive weeks.

1977: **September 24** SAT scores of freshmen entering college are the lowest in the fifty-one years of the test's existence.

1977: **September 26** Freddie Laker begins his no-frills New York-to-London Skytrain air service.

1978: Issac Beshevis Singer wins the Nobel Prize for literature, the second American writer to win in three years.

1978: **March 15** CFCs are banned as spray propellants.

1978: **March 25** A 110-day coal miners' strike, the longest in U.S. history, ends with the signing of a new three-year contract.

1978: **June 28** The U.S. Supreme Court rules in favor of Allen Bakke, who was protesting as unconstitutional the special-admissions policy of the medical school at the University of California at Davis.

1978: **September 17** President Jimmy Carter, Prime Minister Menachem Begin of Israel, and President Anwar Sadat of Egypt end eleven days of discussions at Camp David, Maryland, by signing an accord designed to conclude a peace treaty between Egypt and Israel.

1978: **November 18** Authorities discover the mass suicides and murders of over nine hundred members of Jim Jones's Peoples Temple cult in Guyana.

1979: Jerry Falwell organizes the conservative Moral Majority lobby.

1979: **January 1** The United States officially recognizes the People's Republic of China and terminates its mutual defense treaty with Taiwan.

1979: **March 14** Judy Chicago's controversial feminist artwork *The Dinner Party* is first exhibited at the San Francisco Museum of Modern Art.

1979: **March 28** A partial meltdown begins in the reactor at Unit 2 of Three Mile Island nuclear power plant in Harrisburg, Pennsylvania.

1979: **April 3** Jane Byrne is elected Chicago's first female mayor, winning the election by the largest majority since 1901.

1979: **May 9** California begins gas rationing.

1979: **July 11** Skylab falls into the atmosphere, breaking up over Australia and the Indian Ocean.

1979: **July 31** The Chrysler Corporation, the third largest automaker in the United States, requests a $1-billion federal loan to prevent bankruptcy. On November 1, the federal government guarantees a $1.5-billion loan to Chrysler.

1979: **August 15** United Nations ambassador Andrew Young resigns following an uproar caused by his meeting with a representative of the Palestine Liberation Organization, a meeting that violated U.S. Middle East policy.

1979: **August 15** The Ann Arbor, Michigan, school board approves a program to teach "Black English" to all twenty-eight teachers at Martin Luther King Elementary.

1979: **November 4** In Tehran, Iran, several hundred Iranian militants storm the U.S. embassy and seize the diplomatic personnel. The militants announce they will release the hostages when the United States returns the former shah of Iran, who is recovering from medical treatment in a New York hospital.

The 1970s: An Overview

Many historians and others dismiss the 1970s as the decade that never happened. They view it simply as the period when the political and cultural trends of the 1960s, that decade of tremendous social change, finally came to an end with the rise of those trends that would come to dominate American life in the 1980s, a decade of style and little substance. Feminism, drugs, progressive education, busing, exotic religions, ethnic politics, long hair, blue jeans, and platform shoes lingered from the 1960s. Conservatism, cowboys, televangelists, flag-waving, energy saving, rising cost of living, Sun Belt shift, cocaine, and acid rain foreshadowed the 1980s.

The 1970s, it seemed, had little to define it, except, perhaps, the N.G. Slater Corporation's ever-present "smile button" (created in 1968). Two black, blank eyes and a wide grin superimposed on a yellow sun, the smiley face was an image found on everything everywhere in the decade: lapel buttons, bumper stickers, T-shirts, wall posters, toilet seats. Blissful, welcoming, and optimistic, the smiley face was the perfect expression for such a traumatic decade. Profoundly shaken, the nation was in the midst of a collective repression, yet it tried to act as if nothing had happened.

In fact, much did happen during the 1970s. The Vietnam War, the conflict in Southeast Asia in which the United States had been involved since the 1950s, finally came to an end for Americans in 1973. The peace treaty the U.S. government agreed to was little more than a piece of paper indicating an inglorious defeat. The war, fought for so long at such a great cost for so little gain, had divided the country as nothing had since the American Civil War (1861–65). Antiwar protests filled city streets and college campuses, giving rise to an anger that left Americans dead at the hands of their fellow countrymen.

While the trauma of Vietnam forced Americans to question the role of their government in foreign affairs, the presidency of Richard M. Nixon (1913–1994) forced Americans to question their belief in their government. Paranoid and secretive, ruthless and distrustful, Nixon had been elected in 1968 on the promise of ending America's involvement in the war. In reality, he escalated it, drawing out the conflict for another four years. He sought to open relations with the Soviet Union and Communist China, but his impressive political skills were forever stained by his desire to control and crush his political opponents. The 1972 break-in of the offices of the Democratic National Committee in the Watergate complex led back to the Oval Office and to the president. Facing certain impeachment for his involvement in the illegal activities, Nixon resigned the office of the presidency on August 9, 1974, becoming the first president in the history of the United States to do so.

Of course, not all famous people during the decade were known because of scandals. Ralph Nader and Cesar Chavez tirelessly defended the interests of U.S. consumers and farmworkers. Journalist Gloria Steinem publicized the plight of women with sympathy and intelligence. Donald A. Henderson of the World Health Organization oversaw the eradication of small pox. Muhammad Ali returned from political adversity to become once again "the Greatest" boxer. Billie Jean King used her position as a tennis champion to open avenues for other women to follow.

Such visible, symbolic heroes, however, were the exception in the 1970s. More often, real heroes took a low-key approach to problems, working at the local level for small victories. Typical of such individuals was twenty-seven-year-old homemaker Lois Gibbs of Love Canal, New York, a residential neighborhood near Niagara Falls. When noxious fluids began seeping into basements causing homeowners and their families to fall ill, she organized a grassroots campaign that exposed the area as a toxic waste site. Because of her rallying efforts, the federal government designated Love Canal an emergency area, and the state of New York paid to have residents moved.

Unfortunately, many Americans retreated from public life in the decade, preferring one that was more self-involved. Looking good, feeling right, and eating healthily were ritualistic preoccupations of millions during the "me decade." Magazines, paperbacks, pop music, television, and movies were filled with discussions of sensitivity and feelings. Disco, the pulsating dance music that dominated nightclubs across the country, provided many with an escape from the political, economic, and social problems they clearly did not want to face. However, the me decade of the 1970s would give way to the 1980s, a decade preoccupied with glamour and wealth.

chapter one

Arts and Entertainment

Chronology

1970: *American Top 40,* a weekly countdown of hits on the pop music charts hosted by Casey Kasem, debuts on nationwide radio.

1970: Future Nobel laureate Toni Morrison publishes her first novel, *The Bluest Eye.*

1970: May 2 Mississippi educational television bans *Sesame Street* for its racial content. The State Commission for Educational TV reverses the decision on May 24.

1971: Margaret Harris conducts the Chicago Symphony, becoming the first African American woman to lead a major orchestra.

1971: January 12 *All in the Family,* produced by Norman Lear, debuts on television as a mid-season replacement series.

1971: May 17 The rock musical *Godspell,* written by Michael Tebelak and Stephen Schwartz, opens on Broadway.

1971: October 12 The rock musical *Jesus Christ Superstar,* written by Andrew Lloyd Webber and Tim Rice, opens on Broadway.

1972: March 15 *The Godfather,* Francis Ford Coppola's film adaptation of the best-selling novel by Mario Puzo, opens in movie theaters.

1972: July Actress Jane Fonda arrives in Hanoi, North Vietnam, to begin a two-week tour of the country, during which she will denounce American political and military leaders as "war criminals."

1972: July The first regular issue of *Ms.* magazine, founded by Gloria Steinem, Pat Carbine, and others, hits the newsstands.

1973: Erica Jong publishes her first novel, the controversial and groundbreaking *Fear of Flying.*

1973: March The English rock group Pink Floyd releases its landmark album *The Dark Side of the Moon.* It remains on the *Billboard* Top 200 Albums chart for 741 weeks.

1973: December 26 *The Exorcist,* based on the best-selling novel of the same name by William Peter Blatty, debuts in theaters. The terrifying film initially created mass hysteria, causing some viewers to faint.

1974: The "garage" band the Ramones, whose fast, three-chord sound ushers in the American punk rock movement, begins playing at the New York City club CBGB.

1974: Disco, a beat-driven dance music popular in the black and gay communities, finds mainstream success with hits such as "Rock the Boat," "Rock Your Baby," and "Kung Fu Fighting."

1974: **March 4** The first issue of *People* magazine, an offshoot of *Time* magazine focusing on celebrities and "real life" stories, hits the newsstands.

1975: *The Rocky Horror Picture Show,* an off-beat musical about a Transylvanian transvestite, is released and soon gains cult status.

1975: **January 5** The all-black musical *The Wiz* opens on Broadway, eventually tallying 1,672 performances.

1975: **May 21** *A Chorus Line* debuts at the Newman Theater in New York City.

1976: American writer Saul Bellow wins the Nobel Prize for literature.

1976: The exhibit *Two Centuries of Black American Art* opens at the Los Angeles County Museum of Art.

1976: **September 26** *The Muppet Show* debuts on syndicated television.

1977: **February 20** Alex Haley's *Roots* is listed by *The New York Times* as the top-selling book in the country for twenty consecutive weeks.

1977: **May 25** *Star Wars,* directed by George Lucas, opens in thirty-two movie theaters across the country.

1977: **August 19** Singer Elvis Presley dies of heart failure at the age of forty-two.

1977: **December** *Saturday Night Fever,* a movie starring John Travolta, is released and quickly becomes a popular phenomenon.

1978: Issac Bashevis Singer wins the Nobel Prize for literature, becoming the second American writer to win in three years.

1978: **January** The English punk rock band the Sex Pistols breaks up in the middle of its first American tour when singer Johnny Rotten quits the band.

1978: **January 4** The top-selling paperback in the country, *Close Encounters of the Third Kind,* is a novelization of the film script.

1978: **May 9** *Ain't Misbehavin',* an all-black musical featuring the music of Fats Waller, opens on Broadway, eventually racking up 1,604 performances.

1979: The first digitally recorded album, Ry Cooder's *Bop Till You Drop,* is released.

1979: **March 14** Judy Chicago's controversial feminist artwork *The Dinner Party* is first exhibited at the San Francisco Museum of Modern Art.

1979: **September 15** Massachusetts adopts the nation's first lottery to support the arts.

Overview

At the beginning of the 1970s, American society was still reeling from the political, social, and artistic upheavals of the 1960s. Artists and the public alike were experiencing unprecedented (never before seen) freedom and breaking all sorts of taboos. Change was occurring so rapidly there seemed to be little left that artists had not tried or audiences had not seen. Many critics declared that the novel was dead and that pop art had peaked. Films lost their audiences to the allure of television. And popular music, one of the great unifying cultural forces of the 1960s, began to lose its impact as its fans broke apart into small factions.

Despite the supposed death of many art forms, signs of new life sprouted throughout the decade. The ongoing civil rights movement helped minority artists to emerge as serious voices with which to be reckoned. Indeed, the 1970s marked the arrival of African American artists and entertainers into mainstream arts culture. Their performances fostered a sense of pride and identity in the black community.

At the beginning of the decade, several "blaxploitation" films were marketed as cinema created by and for African Americans. Contrary to expectations, these low-budget films were rejected by many in the black community as stereotypical and demeaning. Soon, serious actors such as James Earl Jones, Cicely Tyson, and Paul Winfield starred in emotional dramas to widespread critical acclaim.

Literature saw the emergence of African American women authors such as Alice Walker and Toni Morrison, who would eventually be awarded the Nobel Prize. The black artistic phenomenon of the decade, however, was Alex Haley's historical narrative *Roots,* which won a special Pulitzer Prize and became the best-selling novel of 1976. The following year, *Roots* was transformed into a highly rated television miniseries that captivated many Americans.

The two significant musical movements of the 1970s, punk rock and disco, could not have sounded more different from one another. Yet they were born in the same place: the New York underground. Punks, originating in the "garage" bands of the 1960s, were fed up with the mainstream melodies that had come to dominate popular music. In response, they played a fast, loud, and lean style of music that contained lyrics laced with images of alienation, rebellion, and violence. On the other hand, disco featured a pulsing, sexual dance beat underneath catchy melodies and lush, percussive arrangements. This dance music reigned supreme in black, Latino, and gay nightclubs and eventually spread into mainstream culture. Disco encouraged escapism with its rhythmic, repetitive music and erotic appeal.

Movies, which had been steadily losing viewers to television, rebounded in the 1970s with the new phenomenon of the blockbuster commercial film. *The Godfather,* released in 1972, started the trend of big box-office records. Audiences turned out in droves to see disaster films, horror movies, science fiction films, Vietnam War dramas, comedies, violent action pictures, and "buddy" movies. All these genres were dominated, however, by the runaway success of just two pictures, directed by young filmmakers Steven Spielberg and George Lucas. Spielberg's *Jaws,* released in 1975, was a true phenomenon, but Lucas's *Star Wars,* released in 1977, revolutionized special effects and changed concepts of movie merchandising. Together, these young directors created a new demand by the public and film producers for ever-bigger blockbusters.

Francis Ford Coppola (1939–) Film director and screenwriter Francis Ford Coppola created three epic films in the 1970s that ensured his place in cinematic history. In 1972, Coppola transformed Mario Puzo's novel *The Godfather* into an award-winning, moneymaking sensation. Two years later, he released *The Godfather: Part II,* a sequel many critics hailed as the second half of one of America's greatest films. In 1979, Coppola released *Apocalypse Now,* his vision of the Vietnam War. Critics either praised it as the ultimate picture of war or panned it as unrealistic. ***Photo reproduced by permission of Archive Photos/Hammond.***

Jane Fonda (1937–) In the 1970s, actress Jane Fonda became known more for her social protests than for her screen presence. She championed the human rights of Native Americans, publicly supported the Black Panthers, and embraced the women's movement. Her highly publicized trip to North Vietnam in 1972 to protest America's involvement in the Vietnam War proved to be too much for many U.S. citizens, who accused Fonda of treason. Fonda reappeared in films in 1978, winning a best actress Oscar for her role in *Coming Home* (ironically, a film about a Vietnam veteran's return to America after the war). ***Photo reproduced by permission of Archive Photos, Inc.***

Jim Henson (1936–1990) Jim Henson had created his first Muppet, Kermit, back in 1959. It wasn't until the premiere of the television show *Sesame Street* ten years later, however, that his work enchanted children in America and beyond. During the 1970s, his puppet creations—including Kermit the Frog, Bert and Ernie, Big Bird, Miss Piggy, and the Cookie Monster—appeared as guests on other television shows and specials. In 1976, *The Muppet Show* debuted on the small screen, becoming an award-winning hit. Three years later, the Muppets made the leap to the big screen in *The Muppet Movie,* the first of several successful films. ***Photo reproduced by permission of the Corbis Corporation.***

Norman Lear (1922–) Television producer Norman Lear changed the nature of American television comedy in the 1970s with his many long-running shows. Focusing on contemporary social topics such as racism and sexism, they were often controversial. His first, and most memorable, comedy was *All in the Family.* Introduced in 1971, the highly popular, Emmy-winning show about a working-class family headed by Archie Bunker, a loudmouthed bigot, was broadcast throughout the decade. Other Lear creations in the 1970s included *Sanford and Son, Maude, Good Times,* and *The Jeffersons.* ***Photo reproduced by permission of AP/Wide World Photos.***

Toni Morrison (1931–) Writer Toni Morrison published her first novel, *The Bluest Eye,* to critical acclaim in 1970. Hailed as a significant new voice in fiction, Morrison sought to document the struggles of African Americans, and especially African American women, to help them connect with their cultural history. With each successive novel, she gained greater critical respect and a larger reading audience. *Song of Solomon,* published in 1977, won the National Book Critics' Circle Award for fiction and became a bestseller. Sixteen years and three more novels later, she was awarded the Nobel Prize for literature in 1993. ***Reproduced by permission of AP/Wide World Photos.***

Richard Pryor (1940–) Actor and comedian Richard Pryor combined his street humor and high-strung nervous energy to become a film and comedic sensation. He appeared in fourteen films in the 1970s, including *Lady Sings the Blues* (1972), *Silver Streak* (1976), and *Greased Lightning* (1977). Critics praised many of his film roles. Throughout the decade, Pryor released million-selling comedy albums, some of which won Grammy awards. His live comedy performances often sold out, and his 1979 concert film, *Richard Pryor Live,* grossed more than thirty million dollars. ***Photo reproduced by permission of AP/Wide World Photos.***

Gloria Steinem (1934–) Gloria Steinem began the 1970s as an admired magazine writer and ended the decade as one of its most respected and influential magazine editors and proponents of women's rights. In 1971, she and others created the National Women's Political Caucus, which promoted feminist issues and encouraged women to run for political office. The following year, Steinem helped found *Ms.* magazine, a publication that challenged mainstream thinking about women's roles in society. It became one of the most successful and talked-about magazines of the 1970s and beyond. ***Photo reproduced by permission of AP/Wide World Photos.***

Donna Summer (1949–) Singer and songwriter Donna Summer helped launch the disco revolution in 1975 with "Love to Love You Baby," the title track on her debut album. Her soulful and sultry vocal style earned her three hit albums by 1977. The following year, she appeared as an aspiring singer in the dance-oriented film *Thank God It's Friday,* and she also sang the movie's award-winning theme song, "Last Dance." Summer's eclectic 1979 double album, *Bad Girls,* which featured disco, rock, blues, ballad, and pop songs, produced three smash hits. ***Photo reproduced by permission of the Corbis Corporation.***

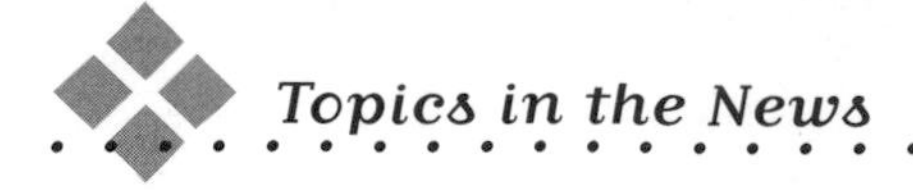

ART: AFRICAN AMERICAN AND WOMEN ARTISTS GAIN PROMINENCE

During the Civil Rights movement of the 1960s, African Americans sought political and social freedom. By the beginning of the 1970s, they were seeking cultural recognition as well. A new group identity and pride in one's heritage were sweeping over racial and ethnic minorities, and African American artists expressed those feelings in their art. They then sought venues that would exhibit their works.

In 1967, African American collage artist and painter Romare Bearden had codirected an exhibition of 150 years of African American art, the most extensive show on the subject ever presented to that time. A few years later, he helped organize a nonprofit gallery in New York City where minority artists could show their works. Other galleries and mainstream museums followed his lead, responding to public demand that works of African American artists be recognized. In 1976, New York City's Metropolitan Museum of Art produced a show titled *Selections of Nineteenth-Century Afro-American Art,* which included never-before-seen works by African American portrait painters and landscape artists. The exhibition also attempted to document slave artifacts as important early artwork.

African American painters in the 1970s also published their work in the new quarterly magazine *Black Art,* and they received support from the newly founded organization Women, Students, and Artists for Black Art Liberation. This group was cofounded in 1970 by African American visual artist Faith Ringgold, whose own work included soft sculptures and story quilts depicting narrative images and original stories from African American history, and life-sized, African-style masks.

Other black artists often incorporated African symbols and traditional colors (red, black, and green) in their work. Charles Searles rendered the vivid life of the African marketplace in *Filas for Sale* (1972), and he evoked the spirit of ritual dance in *Dancer Series* (1975). In *Black Face and Arm Unit* (1971), Ben Jones addressed the importance of body adornment and masks in African culture.

African American female artists in the 1970s, like Faith Ringgold, often found themselves straddling an artistic fence. While addressing the black experience, they also wanted to communicate a feminist message of independence and the importance of realizing one's full potential. In the 1970s, feminism, or the women's rights movement, became the most significant social movement in the country. As women in general tried to change the sexist attitudes of society, so women artists tried to change the sexist attitudes of the art world.

Similar to the experiences of African American male artists, women artists often found their works excluded from heralded museums at the beginning of the decade. In response, groups of artists banded together and opened galleries that showcased the artistic work of women. They also founded magazines like *Heresis,* a feminist publication on art and politics.

Many women artists created work protesting the male-dominated views of history and modern society. Edwina Sandys's bronze sculpture *Christa* (1975) depicted the crucified savior as a woman. Nancy Spero's collage *Torture in Chile* (1974) was an open protest against the treatment of women in the Bueno Pastor jail in that South American country.

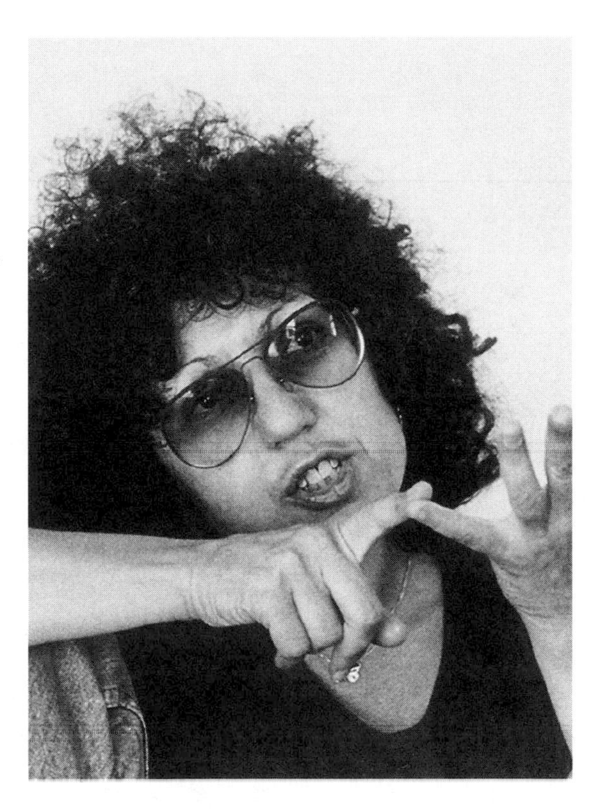

Painter and sculptor Judy Chicago, artist of The Dinner Party, *the best-known piece of feminist artwork of the 1970s.* ***Reproduced by permission of AP/Wide World Photos.***

Perhaps the best-known feminist work of the decade was *The Dinner Party* (1979) by painter and sculptor Judy Chicago. This monumental work features a huge triangular dinner table, forty-six feet long on each side. Thirty-nine place settings, each of which features a wine goblet, cutlery, and an individually sculpted and painted china plate, adorn the table. These items sit on runners of white linen cloth edged in gold and embroidered using needlework techniques taken from history. Each place setting is dedicated to and describes the life of a famous woman in history or mythology. In addition, the table sits on a floor made of twenty-three hundred handmade porcelain tiles, which are inscribed with the names of 999 other women of achievement. It took Chicago six years to complete this elaborate work, which seeks to convey the struggle for freedom and justice waged by women throughout history.

FICTION: BEST-SELLERS AND MINORITY VOICES

Steamy sex, corporate greed, fabulous wealth, global intrigue, romance, and horror—American readers in the 1970s could not seem to get enough of these themes that filled the pages of best-sellers. From Harold Robbins's *The Betsy* (1971) to James Clavell's *Shogun* (1975) to Colleen McCullough's *The Thorn Birds* (1977), the decade was full of epic dramatic novels.

Many of those big novels, such as Peter Benchley's *Jaws* (1974), also became big movies. Others were turned into television miniseries, a popular trend that began with Irwin Shaw's *Rich Man, Poor Man* (1970). By the late 1970s, new books by best-selling authors were being planned simultaneously as hardcovers, paperbacks, and movies or miniseries. Inevitably, the book-to-movie process began to reverse itself: The novelizations of screenplays from blockbuster films such as *The Omen* (1976) and *Close Encounters of the Third Kind* (1977) became popular books after the box-office success of the movies.

While the novel as entertainment soared in the 1970s, the novel as art form seemed to collapse. Many critics and readers believed a different force was needed to invigorate American fiction; as the decade progressed, they looked to minority writers.

The 1960s had seen a rise in African American poetry and fiction, but most of the writers producing that work were men. In the 1970s, however, African American women authors gained acclaim. Toni Morrison's first novel, *The Bluest Eye* (1970), describes a young black girl who dreams of having the features of a white girl. Morrison's strongest work of the decade, *Song of Solomon* (1977), was a complex study of black family life and the search for love and meaning in family history. Other African American female writers also focused on personal and social identity. In *A Hero Ain't Nothin' but a Sandwich,* Alice Childress depicted urban ghetto life with a strong sense of social commitment. Alice Walker's *Meridian* (1976) presented its heroine's search for self as a struggle for racial and gender identity.

The struggle for women writers to define themselves and their community helped create unique works in the 1970s. Erica Jong's *Fear of Flying* (1973) was revolutionary in its explicit handling of a female character's sexual adventures. The novel was equally frank about the character's family and career conflicts. The main character in Judith Rossner's *Looking for Mr. Goodbar* (1975) also cannot come to terms with her ambitions, her sense of suffocation within her family, and her attraction to sexual danger. The character of the wife in Marilyn French's *The Women's Room* (1977) feels oppressed by her domineering husband and eventually leaves to examine the possibilities of self-reliance. Among the issues that the novel explores are female friendships and lesbian relationships as alternatives to traditional marriage.

Besides women authors, critics also recognized Latin American male writers for providing the decade with a distinctive new energy in fiction. In the 1950s and 1960s, Argentinian Jorgé Luis Borges had become the first Latin American writer to achieve an international reputation. In the 1970s, he was followed by Mexican Carlos Fuentes and Colombian

Bestselling Fiction of the 1970s

Year	Title	Author
1970	*Love Story*	Erich Segal
1971	*Wheels*	Arthur Hailey
1972	*Jonathon Livingston Seagull*	Richard Bach
1973	*Jonathon Livingston Seagull*	Richard Bach
1974	*Centennial*	James A. Michener
1975	*Ragtime*	E. L. Doctorow
1976	*Trinity*	Leon Uris
1977	*The Silmarillion*	J. R. R. Tolkien
1978	*Chesapeake*	James A. Michener
1979	*The Matarese Circle*	Robert Ludlum

Gabriel García Márquez. In his historical novel *Terra Nostra,* Fuentes used elements of mystery, myth, and ritual to create a layered sense of time and character. Like Fuentes, García Márquez infused his stories with a lyric sense of ancestry and mystical possibility. His *One Hundred Years of Solitude,* published in 1967 and translated into English in 1970, became the best-selling Latin American novel in the United States.

PUNK ROCK AND DISCO GIVE POPULAR MUSIC A SHOT IN THE ARM

In the 1960s, rock music had appeared to peak in creativity, influence, and range, uniting youthful audiences with its social, political, and cultural relevance. As in the previous decade, the 1970s continued to value the contributions of the singer-songwriter. Although descended from the tradition of 1960s folk singers, these artists sang not of political protest or enlightenment, but of personal confusion, frustration, and loss. The songs of musicians such as James Taylor, Carole King, and Jackson Browne mirrored American society's own move away from social ideals to personal goals.

The 1970s' cultural shift also began to erode the sense of musical unity. Rock music splintered into various styles, such as anthem rock,

Members of the heavy metal band Kiss were famous not only for their music, but also for their stage theatrics and wild makeup. ***©Lynn Goldsmith/Corbis. Reproduced by permission of the Corbis Corporation.***

glam rock, progressive rock, southern rock, California rock, and heavy metal, each of which sought a different audience.

The wide variety of rock music genres produced only a handful of stars. Blockbuster albums, corporate-sponsored tours, and progressive radio formats helped these select musicians make more money than ever before. Often their fame was earned not just from their music, but also

"Jesus" Rock

The themes of peace and love that marked popular music in the late 1960s expanded into a love of the divine when the Beatles' George Harrison released "My Sweet Lord" in 1970. The number-one hit song soon inspired other God-themed hits. In 1971, the Canadian group Ocean topped the charts with "Put Your Hand in the Hand (of the Man from Galilee)." That same year, two musicals appeared on Broadway that were based on the life of Jesus of Nazareth, *Godspell* and *Jesus Christ Superstar.* Each produced a pop music hit: "Day by Day" from *Godspell* and "I Don't Know How to Love Him" from *Jesus Christ Superstar.* Other holy hits during the early 1970s included the movie theme "One Tin Soldier" from *Billy Jack* and the Doobie Brothers' eulogy "Jesus Is Just Alright[sic]." In 1974, Janet Mead, an Australian nun, recorded a rocked-up version of "The Lord's Prayer," which sold more than one-and-one-half million copies worldwide.

As the decade progressed, however, the public seemed more attuned to rock band Judas Priest than Jesus Christ, and religious rock faded. But in 1977, Debby Boone single-handedly revived the trend with her Grammy-winning megahit "You Light up My Life." Boone claimed she sang her song, the longest-running number-one single of the decade, directly to God.

from the way they looked and acted on stage. For example, heavy metal musicians Alice Cooper and the band Kiss used stage theatrics, makeup, and violent images to portray themselves as counterculture icons.

Another symbol of cultural rebellion, the punk rock movement, emerged in the mid-1970s. With its primitive, stripped-down assault of guitars, bass, and drums played fast and loud, punk rock was a refreshing revelation to some, but obnoxious noise to others. Either way, punk musicians could not have cared less. They valued seizing the moment, discarding history, breaking the rules, inventing new ones, and taking a stand (even a wrong one) whenever possible. Punk rock celebrated being young.

Punk first arose in New York City's East Village in the late 1960s in the sounds of the Velvet Underground (with Lou Reed), the Stooges (with Iggy Pop), and the New York Dolls. By the time these groups disbanded in the early 1970s, they had inspired a New York underground rock scene. In 1974, a Bowery bar owner opened his club to rock acts, and CBGB was

A Chorus Line on Broadway

Tony Stevens and Michon Peacock, two Broadway dancers, were tired of bad parts, bad shows, and a lack of respect. In 1974, they turned to choreographer and director Michael Bennett with the thought of forming a new dance company whose productions would showcase company members. Bennett, who had wanted to make his mark on Broadway with something unique, was intrigued by the idea. He contacted dancers who might be interested in such a venture and who might have ideas about future material.

Bennett assembled a large group of dancers, and during a twelve-hour meeting, he had them pour out their life stories: some were tragic, some were comic, and most were a mixture of the two. Bennett taped the confessions. Sensing he had raw material for something new on the musical stage, he decided to work them into a musical about the life of a dancer.

Bennett interviewed more dancers and worked, bit by bit, to put the show together. Everyone in the company contributed material. Some of the

born, offering a venue for bands in the growing punk movement. The definitive New York punk band was the Ramones. Musically limited (and that was the point), they unleashed primitive three-chord songs like "Blitzkrieg Bop" and "Now I Wanna Sniff Some Glue."

In 1976, the Ramones toured England, and, according to many critics, ignited the punk rock movement in that country. Other critics believe British punk rock was an eruption of pent-up rage against the royalty, class distinctions, the establishment, and poor economic conditions in England. British punk was anti-everything, and the ultimate British punk band was the Sex Pistols, formed in 1975. Led by singer Johnny Rotten and bassist Sid Vicious, their hair spiked and their clothing ripped, the Sex Pistols opened the floodgates for loud, fast bands with screaming numbers such as "Anarchy in the U.K." and "God Save the Queen." In contrast, however, some British punk bands, like the Clash, tried to give their lyrics social relevance and promote political change.

By the end of the decade, punk had begun to fizzle out. The Sex Pistols broke up in 1978 in the middle of their first American tour; Johnny

dancers performed their own monologues; others were assigned segments that had been rewritten and restructured. Finally, the story for the show came together: At an audition for an upcoming Broadway production, a director and a choreography assistant choose seventeen dancers. The director tells them he is looking for a strong dancing chorus of four men and four women, and he wants to learn more about them. They are then told to talk about themselves.

The real-life tensions and deeply personal material made *A Chorus Line* unique. The basic idea, to let each dancer tell his or her own story, had never been tried before. Finally, after eighteen months of work, *A Chorus Line* opened on Broadway in May 1975. It was an instant box-office smash, receiving rave reviews from critics and audiences. Among its many accolades were nine Tony Awards and the 1976 Pulitzer Prize for drama. The show played for fifteen years on Broadway, entertaining almost seven million theatergoers.

Rotten later announced that punk was dead. New wave, a pop-driven offshoot of punk, began to gain mainstream success. Bands with skinny ties and artsy attitudes soon topped the pop charts. Angered by the commercialization of its sound, punk went back underground, only to emerge in the early 1990s in the Pacific Northwest in a different form: grunge.

Whereas punk was a shot in the arm for rock, disco was a shot in the arm for dance music. First popularized in urban black, Latino, and gay clubs, disco restored a dance groove to a faltering style. Its sound was purely escapist, with a pulsing beat beneath catchy melodies and a dense, multilayered arrangement. Flashing lights and a hot, crowded dance floor combined to intensify disco's primary message: sex.

The most popular disco music was produced by African American artists, who began to have commercial success in the summer of 1974 with hits such as "Rock the Boat" and "Rock Your Baby." The following summer, with Van McCoy's classic instrumental "The Hustle," the disco movement became a true phenomenon, and black artists such as the Ohio Players and Chic were at the forefront.

Top Singles of the 1970s

Year	Song	Artist
1970	"Bridge Over Troubled Water"	Simon and Garfunkel
1971	"Joy to the World"	Three Dog Night
1972	"American Pie-Parts I & II"	Don McLean
1973	"Tie a Yellow Ribbon Round the Old Oak Tree"	Tony Orlando and Dawn
1974	"The Way We Were"	Barbra Streisand
1975	"Love Will Keep Us Together"	Captain & Tennille
1976	"Disco Lady"	Johnnie Taylor
1977	"You Light Up My Life"	Debby Boone
1978	"Night Fever"	Bee Gees
1979	"My Sharona"	The Knack

In just a few years, artists everywhere jumped on the disco bandwagon; European groups Silver Connection and ABBA even had chart toppers. By 1977, with the huge success of the film *Saturday Night Fever* and its accompanying soundtrack by the Bee Gees, it seemed as though white pop stars had taken over disco. Despite this trend, the true diva of disco remained an African American: Donna Summer. Her sexy, full-throttle vocals produced many smash hits, from "Love to Love You Baby" to "MacArthur Park" to "Last Dance.".

By 1978, disco was so popular that thirty-six million adults had invaded twenty thousand disco clubs nationwide. More than two hundred radio stations had converted to an all-disco format. Just when it seemed there would be no stopping disco, the inevitable happened. Tired of what they viewed as empty-headed music, millions of rock fans started an antidisco backlash. Although it would continue as a popular musical form in Europe and elsewhere, disco soon lost its luster in mainstream America.

FILM: BLOCKBUSTERS AND BLAXPLOITATION

The Hollywood film industry was in trouble as the 1970s began. Audiences had been shrinking throughout the previous decade as television

John Travolta in a scene from the highly successful 1970s film Saturday Night Fever. ***Reproduced by permission of Archive Photos.***

viewing increased. By the late 1960s, only one film in six was making a profit. By 1971, weekly movie attendance in the United States had reached a low of 17.5 million, down from 80 million viewers a week in Hollywood's peak year of 1946. Yet just one year later, the movie industry's downward spiral was halted by the success of one film: *The Godfather.*

Within a year of its release in 1972, *The Godfather* had broken the previous box-office record held for seven years by *The Sound of Music* (1965). It eventually grossed (earned) almost $135 million. Director Francis Ford

Top Films of 1970s

Year	Film
1970	*Love Story*
1971	*Fiddler on the Roof*
1972	*The Godfather*
1973	*The Exorcist*
1974	*The Towering Inferno*
1975	*Jaws*
1976	*Rocky*
1977	*Star Wars*
1978	*Grease*
1979	*Kramer vs. Kramer*

Coppola's magnificent film adaptation of Mario Puzo's best-selling novel, about a close-knit fictional Mafia crime family in the 1940s, instantly became a part of American culture. Two years later, Coppola directed *The Godfather: Part II,* which critics claimed was as good as or better than the original film. Together, the first two *Godfather* pictures were the most influential movies of the 1970s.

Other blockbusters and their sequels quickly followed. In 1973, *American Graffiti* grossed more than $50 million, while *The Sting* made more than $75 million. Helped by the success of their respective soundtrack albums, both films contributed to a nationwide nostalgia craze. That same year, the horror film *The Exorcist,* a terrifying story about a young girl who is possessed by an evil spirit, raked in more than $85 million. It spawned imitators such as *The Omen* (1976) and *Audrey Rose* (1977).

All of these thrillers were dwarfed by a box-office smash in 1975: director Steven Spielberg's *Jaws,* about a giant shark that terrorizes the waters of a beach community. *Jaws* earned $133 million and touched off a rash of films in which ordinary citizens were threatened by huge bears, alligators, and other wild creatures. The film even spawned three sequels of its own. Spielberg followed *Jaws* with another blockbuster just two years later, *Close Encounters of the Third Kind,* an optimistic and awe-inspiring portrayal of alien encounters.

The Rocky Horror Picture Show

In 1975, a film musical called *The Rocky Horror Picture Show* was released in the United States. The low-budget movie, about a young couple who become unwilling pawns in a mad transvestite (a person who dresses as the opposite sex) scientist's experiment, was an immediate flop. A Broadway version of the movie released the same year was equally disastrous. Despite its poor box office showing, the film soon developed an underground reputation, especially in the gay community, and the film reopened as a midnight movie in New York City. Other midnight screenings in other cities ensued, and a bizarre and unprecedented cult following arose.

The cult audience for *The Rocky Horror Picture Show* included college students, gays, sci-fi (science fiction) addicts, old movie fans, transvestites, punk rockers, and social misfits. Throughout a typical screening, audience members often dressed as the film's characters, shouted the movie's (or their own) dialogue at the screen at appropriate times, sang and danced along with the musical numbers, and threw rice or fired water pistols at relevant moments. The wildly flamboyant audience upstaged the movie, and those people who were seeing the film for the first time (called "virgins") could be irritated or even frightened by the experience.

The phenomenon that *The Rocky Horror Picture Show* had become continued throughout the 1970s and into the following decades.

The biggest box-office hit of the 1970s was director George Lucas's space fantasy tale *Star Wars,* released in 1977. It grossed an unprecedented $175 million and became such a cultural phenomenon that it started a science-fiction movie craze in the late 1970s. Films such as *Superman: The Movie* (1978), *Alien* (1979), *The Black Hole* (1979), and *Star Trek: The Motion Picture* (1979) all followed in its wake. *Star Wars* set a new cinematic standard for special effects, and it forever changed the concept of movie marketing. It remained the highest-grossing film of all time until 1982, when Spielberg's *E.T.: The Extra-Terrestrial* was released.

Science fiction, disaster, horror, nostalgia, comedy—blockbusters and other films of the 1970s largely fell into these categories. Neglected were films about the black experience or films featuring black stars. African American audiences wanted more representation in film, both in front of the camera and behind it. As the Black Power movement blossomed in the late 1960s, movies needed to reflect the reality of African American life.

In the early 1970s African Americans witnessed a wave of films made by blacks for black audiences. Most of these movies, however, presented urban ghetto life in a gritty, unforgiving style. Profanity, violence, and explicit sexuality marked these films. The underlying message was usually a separatist one: Blacks and whites could not, and should not, live together. At the same time, the black characters in the films embraced white capitalist (money-making) values. The heroes were generally cool, fearless superstuds with flashy clothes, sleek cars, and big guns who treated women as casually as money. This tone was set with the release of Melvin Van Peebles's X-rated *Sweet Sweetback's Baadasssss Song* (1971) and Gordon Parks's *Shaft* (1971) and *Superfly* (1972). Although these films were groundbreaking, they relied heavily on sex and violence and, except for *Shaft,* the hero was either a dope dealer or a pimp.

Despite being stereotypical or even absurd, these "blaxploitation" (black exploitation) films made incredible profits. Filmed for less than $500,000 apiece, each of these three films earned as much as $20 million. Starved for any sort of black images on movie screens, black audiences turned out in droves to see the new films. Hollywood took notice of what it believed was an unforeseen gold mine and quickly filled silver screens with black movies. Unfortunately, many of them were increasingly ridiculous: *Blacula* (1972), *Blackenstein* (1973), *Black the Ripper* (1973), *Blackfather* (1973), and *Black Caesar* (1973).

Many African American intellectuals and political leaders criticized these blaxploitation films. They believed the films had neither artistic nor cultural value, offering only violence, reverse racism, and the creation of new stereotypes. They also complained about the films' treatment of women as sex objects to be used and discarded. In response, Gordon Parks said his films were merely fantasy and escapist entertainment that black audiences needed.

By the mid-1970s, the blaxploitation craze had died out. Although comedic films offered the greatest opportunities for black actors and directors during the decade, a few successful dramatic films featured exceptional black performers. James Earl Jones emerged as a leading actor in *The Great White Hope* (1970), which confronted the subject of interracial marriage. Diana Ross stunned audiences with her harsh portrayal of jazz singer Billie Holliday in *Lady Sings the Blues* (1972). And Cicely Tyson and Paul Winfield paired up in *Sounder* (1972), an honest and sensitive story of a struggling black family in the rural South in the 1930s.

Top Television Shows of the 1970s

Year	Show
1970	*Marcus Welby, M.D.*
1971	*All in the Family*
1972	*All in the Family*
1973	*All in the Family*
1974	*All in the Family*
1975	*All in the Family*
1976	*Happy Days*
1977	*Laverne & Shirley*
1978	*Laverne & Shirley*
1979	*60 Minutes*

❖ TELEVISION: SOCIAL RELEVANCE AND THE RISE OF THE MINISERIES

After the social and cultural upheavals of the 1960s, the 1970s seemed less exciting. In the media (magazines, newspapers, radio, and television), however, compelling coverage unfolded during the decade. The media helped to uncover military abuses during the Vietnam War (1954–75) and exposed the corrupt administration of President Richard M. Nixon (1913–1994). Magazines vigorously promoted social reforms as they had not done before. And television, which had been introduced to American society in the late 1940s and was the dominant medium by the 1970s, began airing programs that addressed social concerns.

Commercial television had begun to flirt with socially relevant programs in the late 1960s. In 1968, Dianne Carroll starred as an independent career woman and mother in *Julia,* the first television show featuring an African American lead actor. The following year, the comedy-drama *Room 222* debuted. Set in an integrated Los Angeles high school, the show touched on serious contemporary issues such as racism, drug use, guns in schools, illiteracy, homophobia, and teenage pregnancy.

The show that laid the groundwork for relevant programming in the 1970s was the situation comedy *All in the Family,* which debuted as a mid-

The Rise and Fall of "Family Time" on TV

By the spring of 1974, a public outcry had arisen over the amount of sex, crime, and violence shown on television, especially during prime time (typically from 8:00 P.M. to 10:00 P.M.). With the federal government threatening to step in, the National Association of Broadcasters established a one-hour slot at the beginning of prime time set aside for family-oriented programs. Shows that were deemed inappropriate for viewing were not to be broadcast during what became known as "family time" or "family hour."

From the very beginning, the measure did not reduce the amount of sex and violence broadcast on the small screen. Networks merely rearranged their schedules so that certain shows appeared at other times. Furthermore, writers and producers of television programs were outraged by what they believed were limitations placed on their freedom and creativity. The Writers' Guild of America filed a lawsuit challenging the policy. Norman Lear, the writer-producer of the hugely popular show *All in the Family,* filed another. In 1976, a U.S. District Court judge ruled that the family viewing policy was a violation of the First Amendment, and the policy was abandoned.

season replacement series at the beginning of 1971. Produced by Norman Lear and Bud Yorkin, the show starred Carroll O'Connor as Archie Bunker, a white, working-class dock foreman who supported every negative ethnic and racial stereotype. His family, especially his daughter, Gloria, and her husband, Mike, held liberal, unprejudiced views that often clashed with Archie's. Even his wife, Edith, did not share his opinions. Race relations, feminism, sexuality, abortion, and other controversial issues were discussed on the show openly and sometimes harshly, but always tempered with humor.

For the first few months after *All in the Family* began airing, American audiences were not sure how to respond to the program, and it was almost cancelled. By the summer of 1971, however, the controversial show had captured a growing audience, and it became a hit. It remained in the number-one spot for five straight seasons. During its run, *All in the Family* inspired other popular, socially concerned shows, including *Maude* (1972–78) and *The Jeffersons* (1975–85).

One of the biggest television successes in the 1970s was the miniseries. Such shows, essentially made-for-television movies that extended over more than two nights, attracted millions of viewers. One of the first popular miniseries, ABC's *Rich Man, Poor Man* (1976), proved that such programming could work. No miniseries was more successful or socially relevant, however, than *Roots*.

Broadcast in January 1977 over eight successive nights, the twelve-hour *Roots* epic was based on Alex Haley's nonfiction work of the same name in which he traced his family history from its African origins through years of slavery and emancipation (freedom). Featuring an impressive cast (including newcomer LeVar Burton) and a vast historical sweep, *Roots* captivated an estimated 130 million viewers, with some episodes breaking viewer records. Ordinary people and even members of Congress changed their schedules for a week so as not to miss the next installment.

LeVar Burton in a scene from Roots, *the most successful and socially relevant television miniseries ever to be broadcast.* **Reproduced by permission of AP/Wide World Photos.**

Roots had a significant cultural impact by arousing an unprecedented interest in genealogy (researching family history) in general and African American history in particular. Among other things, the miniseries quietly broke new ground in American television by briefly showing bare-breasted women, the first time a prime-time network other than public television had shown frontal nudity. A fourteen-hour sequel, *Roots: The Next Generations,* which aired in February 1979 and starred James Earl Jones as Haley, was also successful.

For More Information

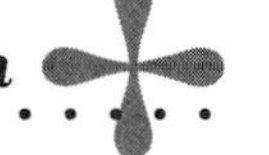

BOOKS

Andriote, John-Manuel. *Hot Stuff: A Brief History of Disco.* New York: Morrow, 2001.

Chicago, Judy. *Beyond the Flower: The Autobiography of a Feminist Artist.* New York: Viking, 1996.

Edelstein, Andrew J., and Kevin McDonough. *The Seventies: From Hot Pants to Hot Tubs.* New York: Dutton, 1990.

Haley, Alex. *Roots: The Saga of an American Family.* New York: Dell, 1980.

McCrohan, Donna. *Archie and Edith, Mike and Gloria: The Tumultuous History of All in the Family.* New York: Workman Publishing, 1988.

McNeil, Legs, and Gillian McCain, eds. *Please Kill Me: The Uncensored Oral History of Punk*. New York: Penguin, 1997.

Morrison, Toni. *Song of Solomon*. New York: Plume, 1987.

WEB SITES

Greatest Films of the 1970s. http://www.filmsite.org/70sintro.html (accessed on February 27, 2002).

In the 70s. http://www.inthe70s.com/index.shtml (accessed on February 27, 2002).

1970s Bestsellers. http://www.caderbooks.com/best70.html (accessed on February 27, 2002).

Seventies Almanac-Year By Year. http://www.geocities.com/SunsetStrip/8678/seventiesalmanac.html (accessed on February 27, 2002).

This Week in 70s History. http://www.70ps.com/week.html (accessed on February 27, 2002).

The Women of 1970s Punk. http://www.comnet.ca/~rina/ (accessed on February 27, 2002).

chapter two Business and the Economy

1970: January 19 Inflation reaches 6.1 percent, the highest rate since the Korean War (1950–53).

1970: March 25 The first major postal workers' strike in American history ends after seven days.

1970: October 26 The federal government mandates the use of unleaded gasoline in federal vehicles.

1970: December 4 The federal government announces that unemployment has risen to 5.8 percent. In response, officials reduce interest rates.

1971: February 6 *Time* magazine reaches an agreement regarding job discrimination with 140 female employees.

1971: March 8 The U.S. Supreme Court prohibits employers from using job tests that discriminate against African Americans.

1971: June 10 President Richard M. Nixon ends a twenty-year trade embargo against Communist China.

1971: December 10 President Richard M. Nixon signs a $25-billion tax cut.

1972: The Dow-Jones average hits 1,000 for the first time in history.

1972: August 15 A U.S. federal court lifts an April 1970 injunction banning the construction of the Trans-Alaska Pipeline.

1972: November 16 PepsiCo announces a deal to sell its products in the Soviet Union.

1973: January 11 The Nixon administration ends mandatory wage and price controls, except in the food, construction, and health-care industries.

1973: May 3 A court order directs Delta Air Lines to open more positions to women and African Americans.

1973: October Following the beginning of the war between Israel and several Arab states, some members of the Organization of Petroleum Exporting Countries (OPEC) begin an embargo of oil exports to the United States and other Western nations.

1973: December 22 To conserve gasoline and improve driving safety, the U.S. Congress orders states to reduce interstate highway speed limits to fifty-five miles per hour.

1974: March 18 Members of OPEC, except Libya and Syria, end their oil embargo of the West.

1974: April 30 President Richard M. Nixon's authority to impose wage and price controls on the American economy ends with the expiration of the 1970 Economic Wage Stabilization Act.

1974: October 8 President Gerald Ford announces his program to control inflation, called Whip Inflation Now (WIN). Despite a denial by President Ford, Federal Reserve Chairman Arthur Burns states that a recession has begun.

1975: Exxon Corporation replaces General Motors as the nation's wealthiest company.

1975: February 7 The federal government reports January unemployment at 8.2 percent, the highest level since 1941.

1975: November 7 The U.S. Supreme Court rules unconstitutional a Utah law denying unemployment benefits to women in the third trimester of pregnancy.

1976: March 26 The federal government accuses the Encyclopaedia Britannica company of deceptive selling and other practices.

1976: September 15 American Bank and Trust Company fails, the fourth largest banking default in history.

1976: December 18 More than 175 U.S. companies admit to offering over $300 million in bribes since 1970.

1977: The United States posts the highest trade deficit in history: $31.1 billion.

1977: Many consumers respond to high coffee prices by switching to tea.

1977: September 26 Freddie Laker begins his no-frills New York-to-London Skytrain airline service.

1977: October 3 Three hundred American Airlines female flight attendants, fired for becoming pregnant between 1965 and 1970, receive a $2.7-million civil rights settlement.

1978: Due to inflation, goods costing $100.00 in 1967 now cost $200.09.

1978: March 25 A 110-day coal miners' strike, the longest in U.S. history, ends with the signing of a new three-year contract.

1979: The Islamic revolution in Iran cuts off Iranian oil exports and leads to widespread oil shortages and soaring energy costs.

1979: The federal government deregulates long-distance phone service.

1979: May 9 California begins gas rationing due to continued scarce supply.

1979: July 31 The Chrysler Corporation, the third largest automaker in the United States, requests a $1-billion federal loan to prevent bankruptcy. On November 1, the federal government guarantees a $1.5-billion loan to Chrysler.

Overview

During the 1970s, business conditions and the economy were the worst they had been in decades. International events, the most important being the oil crises of 1973–74 and 1979, rocked a decade earmarked by rampant wage and price inflation and slow business growth. The unprecedented combination of these negative economic factors led to a new term: "stagflation." It also humbled the large institutions in the United States—the government, big business, labor unions—by demonstrating their reduced ability to affect the economy.

The increasing inflation during the 1970s was brought about in large part because of the government's funding of the Vietnam War and President Lyndon B. Johnson's "Great Society" social welfare programs. President Richard M. Nixon's initial unwillingness to curb the Johnson administration's government spending worsened the situation. As inflation rose, Nixon eventually responded with government-mandated wage-and-price controls, but they were only temporary measures. His presidential successors during that decade, Gerald R. Ford and Jimmy Carter, fared no better in their efforts to keep prices down.

Big businesses in America, particularly the automobile manufacturers, suffered terribly in such a poor economy. General Motors, Ford, and Chrysler were at the mercy of uncontrollable changes in the oil market and consumer preferences. As energy shortages arose in the decade, consumers demanded energy-efficient products, especially cars. Slow to see the need for such products, American carmakers lost ground to their European and Japanese competitors, who were able to satisfy consumer demand more quickly. In order to avoid bankruptcy in late 1979, Chrysler had to be propped up by government loan guarantees. During the decade, other American companies and even New York City also had to be helped by huge federal loans.

In such a depressed economy, it was remarkable that women and minorities continued to make gains in workplace equality. Those gains did not occur because of a change in business attitude toward the workers' abilities, but because of legislation and judicial action. Lawmakers and the courts forced businesses to alter their hiring practices so that everyone could have an equal chance at a successful career. Although by the end of the decade more women were employed than ever before, they continued to earn less money than their male peers earned for the same work. Equality in the workplace was still decades away.

Lost in the turmoil of the 1970s was the fact that the U.S. economy was going through a painful, yet necessary, transformation. Small companies forming at that time would, in the years to come, radically change the U.S. and world economy. Among these were Apple, Microsoft, and Nike. They set the stage for a new type of economy in the future, one that was less dependent on the large manufacturing companies that had dominated America for a large portion of the twentieth century.

Philip Knight (1938–) In 1972, Philip Knight and his former track coach from the University of Oregon, Bill Bowerman, founded the athletic footwear company Nike, named after the Greek goddess of victory. With Nike, the pair began to manufacture and market their own line of imaginatively designed athletic shoes with the distinctive "swoosh" logo. By the end of the decade, with sales nearing $100 million, Nike manufactured nearly half the athletic shoes sold in the country. *Photo reproduced by permission of Nike, Inc.*

Freddie Laker (1922–) English entrepreneur Freddie Laker fought a six-year battle to offer cheap fares on long-distance airline routes. Finally, on September 26, 1977, Laker launched his no-frills, low-cost airline service, called Skytrain, across the North Atlantic. For $102 for a one-way ticket, or $236 for round-trip, passengers could fly between London and New York. Laker's airline offered no advanced booking, limited baggage service, and no free beverage or food service. Despite this, passengers filled his flights, forcing major airlines to offer similar fares. *©Hulton-Deutsch Collection/Corbis. Photo reproduced by permission of the Corbis Corporation.*

Ralph Nader (1934–) Consumer advocate Ralph Nader had been a tireless champion for consumer rights and protections since the 1960s. In 1971, he founded Public Citizen, a national nonprofit public interest organization. Nader and followers of his consumer-rights crusade investigated and attacked corporations they believed manufactured unsafe products. Nader also helped to create the Environmental Protection Agency in 1970 and to draft the Freedom of Information Act in 1974. Early in the decade, he was one of the most prominent and popular figures in the public eye. Despite criticism, Nader continued his watchdog efforts on behalf of the American consumer throughout the following decades. *Photo reproduced by permission of AP/Wide World Photos.*

William Simon (1927–) William Simon was appointed administrator of the new Federal Energy Office (present-day Department of Energy) in December 1973. Relatively unknown, Simon quickly became a household name for the effective way he handled the country's energy resources during the OPEC oil embargo and resulting energy crisis. He urged Americans to conserve energy and sought to wean the United States from its dependence on foreign oil by developing new sources of energy. Programs he developed would prove important in the coming decade. In April 1974, Simon was appointed Secretary of the Treasury, a position he held until 1976. *Photo reproduced by permission of Archive Photos, Inc.*

OIL EMBARGOES AND A DECADE-LONG ENERGY CRISIS

At the beginning of the 1970s, Americans consumed vast amounts of energy compared to citizens of other countries. Although Americans at the time accounted for only 6 percent of the world's population, they used 30 percent of all the energy produced. Americans consumed as much energy in seven days as people in other parts of the world consumed in a year. Car manufacturers continued to make the large sedans and hot rod muscle cars popular since the 1950s. With souped-up engines, these gas-guzzling automobiles had poor fuel economy performance, barely getting ten miles to the gallon. Also, many homes and businesses were poorly designed and insulated, further wasting energy.

Although energy conservation was not a priority, fuel shortages had begun to arise in the United States during the late 1960s. During the hot summer months, some electrical utilities on the East Coast could not build enough capacity to meet the increased consumer demand. They were forced to lower their voltage, resulting in occasional brownouts (temporary dimming of lights due to a reduction in electrical power) in urban areas. Shortages in U.S. resources of coal and natural gas also developed, which led to the temporary shutdown of factories in the Midwest that relied on those fuels to power their machinery.

As energy consumption in the country increased in the 1960s and early 1970s, so did the demand for foreign oil. In 1972, forty-four million barrels of oil were being consumed every day in America, more than double the amount a decade earlier. The oil-producing nations (mostly in the Middle East) had established the Organization of Petroleum Exporting Countries (OPEC) in 1960 to fix crude oil prices. In 1970, taking advantage of the growing oil needs of the United States and other Western nations, the OPEC nations, led by Libya, began to demand a greater share of the profits of Western petroleum refineries located on their soil. These companies then raised oil prices to consumers and the American economy suffered.

To improve the economy, President Richard M. Nixon (1913–1994) took steps to formulate a national energy policy. Among other efforts, he asked the U.S. Congress in 1971 to pass legislation that would promote the development of new fuel sources and encourage energy conservation. Because of the strenuous objection of oil industry lobbyists, passing general energy legislation became a decade-long political nightmare.

The energy problem became an energy crisis when war broke out on October 6, 1973, in the Middle East, source of much of America's oil supply. This war is known by different names in different countries. Israel calls the conflict the Yom Kippur War, named after the Jewish holy day on which the fighting began. Egypt and Syria, Israel's adversaries, and their Arab neighbors refer to it as either the October War or the Ramadan War (Ramadan is the Muslim holy month of fasting). Among other reasons, Egypt and Syria attacked Israel to reclaim territory lost in the previous Arab-Israeli Wars of 1948–49, 1956, and 1967.

Shortly after the war began, OPEC embargoed, or cut off the flow of, oil exports to the United States, Western Europe, and Japan in retaliation for their support of Israel in the conflict. Within weeks, America faced its most critical energy shortage since World War II (1939–45). Although the United States relied on OPEC for only about 15 percent of its oil, that oil was important for industry and transportation. In addition, distributors, businesses, and consumers began to hoard oil and gasoline, causing prices to soar. Retail gasoline prices jumped 40 percent, and around the country Americans found themselves in long lines at gasoline stations.

The oil embargo lasted until March 1974 when peace negotiations progressed between the warring nations. However, the price of a barrel of oil remained more than six times higher than it had been before the conflict. Many Americans abandoned their gas-guzzling, American-made automobiles for fuel-efficient, foreign-made compact cars. This shift in consumer demand led to huge layoffs in the American automobile industry and an increase in America's trade deficit.

As a long-term remedy to the energy crisis, President Nixon announced an ambitious program called Project Independence. The goal of this project was to have the United States become energy self-sufficient by 1980. The technologies to be studied and possibly adopted to meet the goal included solar energy, geothermal energy, wind and hydroelectric power, oil extraction, and nuclear power. Because of the Watergate scandal and his subsequent resignation from office, President Nixon was never able to implement his program.

Gerald R. Ford (1913–), Nixon's successor as president, proposed a ten-year plan to build 200 nuclear-power plants, erect 30 new oil refineries, dig 250 new coal mines, construct 150 coal-fired power plants, and create 20 major synthetic-fuel plants. The U.S. Congress rejected this plan, balking at the high cost. Congress did order new fuel-efficiency standards for American-made automobiles and authorized construction of the Trans-Alaska Pipeline.

OPPOSITE PAGE An aerial view of a line of waiting cars to fill up with gas at an Exxon station in Fort Lee, New Jersey. ***Reproduced by permission of AP/Wide World Photos.***

Part of the problem with addressing the energy crisis in the 1970s was the short attention span of the American public. When the 1973–74 oil embargo reduced supplies and sent prices soaring, Americans complained loudly and adopted certain conservation measures. Afterward, when prices and supplies stabilized slightly, those conservation measures were forgotten quickly. President Ford's energy program in part fell victim to this indifference, and so, too, did that of his successor, Jimmy Carter (1924–).

Trans-Alaska Pipeline

In 1968, the largest oil fields in United States territory were discovered under Prudhoe Bay, an inlet of the Beaufort Sea along Alaska's northern coast. To help combat the growing energy shortage in America, plans were devised to build a pipeline that would carry the oil across the state from the Arctic North Slope to the ice-free south Alaska port of Valdez. After settling land claims with Native American tribes in Alaska, over the bitter objections of environmentalists, the U.S. Congress authorized construction of the Trans-Alaska Pipeline on July 17, 1973.

Building of the pipeline began on March 27, 1975. During the height of its construction, over twenty thousand people worked on the pipeline. By the time it was completed on May 31, 1977, $8 billion had been spent on its construction. Oil began to flow through the pipeline less than a month later, on June 20, and the first tanker carrying that oil left the Valdez port on August 1 of that year.

The pipeline is a tube of steel 48 inches in diameter. It is wrapped with four inches of fiberglass insulation covered with a coat of aluminum sheet metal. Because much of Alaska is covered with permafrost (permanently

More so than his predecessors, President Carter responded to the U.S. energy crisis. Within ninety days of his inauguration in 1977, he introduced an energy policy that was a mix of programs. President Carter wanted gas and oil prices, which had been regulated or controlled by the federal government since the Nixon administration, to be free to respond to supply and demand. He also wanted to create incentives for businesses to develop alternative energy sources such as gasohol, a mixture of gasoline and ethyl alcohol produced from corn. In October of that year, President Carter established the Department of Energy.

However, the U.S. Congress whittled down President Carter's program for weaning the United States from foreign oil to virtually nothing. At the time, 70 percent of all U.S. oil imports came from OPEC countries. The lack of a clear energy policy proved costly in early 1979 when a revolution in Iran brought that country's oil exports to a halt. The remaining OPEC members then raised prices, and a second oil panic was underway. Once again, large oil companies hoarded oil, further driving supplies downward

frozen soil lying beneath the ground surface), over half of the pipeline is above ground, supported by posts. From Prudhoe Bay to Valdez, the pipeline runs nearly 800 miles, crossing three mountain ranges and hundreds of rivers and streams.

Because it is pumped from thousands of feet below ground, the oil is very hot when it reaches the surface of Prudhoe Bay. Heat exchangers cool the oil to about 120°F, then pumps send it through the pipeline at a speed of about 5.5 miles per hour. The journey from Prudhoe Bay to Valdez takes about six days. Over one million barrels of oil travel through the pipeline each day.

In 1976, Alaskans approved an amendment to their state constitution creating the Alaska Permanent Fund. Twenty-five percent of all royalty income the state receives from the pipeline revenue goes into the fund, which would provide Alaska with income when and if the oil stops flowing. Beginning in 1982, a portion of the interest income from the Permanent Fund was distributed to all eligible residents of Alaska. Yearly dividends paid to Alaskans have ranged from just over $300 to almost $2,000.

and prices upward. Lines at gas stations returned, and the American economy was thrown into a recession (period of decline in economic trade and prosperity), one of the most severe in decades.

Nuclear power was proposed by many policy makers as a possible solution to the energy crisis. Hope dimmed just a few months later, however, when the reactor at the Three Mile Island nuclear power plant in Pennsylvania suffered a meltdown. The American public's view of nuclear power was forever tainted, and the search for alternative energy sources would continue in the following decades.

A COUNTRY PARALYZED BY INFLATION AND STAGNATION

The decade of the 1970s was the most traumatic for the American economy since the Great Depression (a period of severe economic decline in the United States from 1929 to 1941). Coming after twenty-five years of consistent prosperity and growth, the downturn of the economy hit with

The Truth Is in the Labeling

In the early 1970s, U.S. consumers wanted assurances that advertising claims were truthful, that product weights and measures were accurate, and that the goods they bought were safe. Because the economic fortunes of the nation depended on the reliability of American goods and the satisfaction of the American consumer, the federal government responded.

In October 1972, President Richard M. Nixon signed the Consumer Product Safety Act, which authorized an independent commission to establish safeguards against unsafe household items, food, drugs, and cosmetics. The Consumer Product Safety Commission is regarded as the most powerful independent federal agency ever created by the federal government. That same year, Congress also passed legislation protecting automobile buyers against false claims and requiring pharmaceutical companies to reveal information about themselves and their products.

In 1973, the Food and Drug Administration, a division of the U.S. Department of Health, Education, and Welfare, required labeling on packaged food to inform consumers of nutritional value and potentially harmful ingredients. Foods making nutritional claims had to list on their labels the U.S. Recommended Daily Allowance (RDA) of protein and of seven essential vitamins, in addition to their fat content and caloric value.

especially powerful force. Productivity was down, costs were up, unemployment soared, inflation was high, exports were low, and imports swamped the market. Nearly every economic indicator went down during the decade.

The administrations of all three presidents in the decade—Nixon, Ford, and Carter—tried a variety of creative approaches to revive the economy, but most failed. Although the causes behind the economic decline of the 1970s are numerous and controversial, two results are of primary importance: the federal deficit and trade balances.

The Vietnam War (1954–75) had badly burdened the American economy. President Lyndon B. Johnson (1908–1973) and his administration had funded the war by borrowing and printing money, raising the national debt (the total amount of money owed by the federal government as a result of

American Nobel Prize Winners in Economics

Year	Economist
1970	Paul A. Samuelson
1971	Simon Kuznets
1972	Kenneth J. Arrow
1973	Wassily Leontief
1974	No award given to an American
1975	Tjalling C. Koopmans
1976	Milton Friedman
1977	No award given to an American
1978	Herbert A. Simon
1979	Theodore W. Schultz

borrowing) to an unprecedented $436 billion by 1972. This also sparked runaway inflation, defined as the general price increase of goods and services resulting from an excess supply of available money relative to those goods and services. Since key American industries had to devote much of their resources to military research and development, they fell behind their Japanese and European competitors in the research and development of consumer goods. In addition, since much effort and material were devoted to the war effort, prices for labor (wages) and goods were driven higher.

While the Vietnam War was the greatest single component of public spending at the beginning of the 1970s, it alone did not add to the American debt. The social welfare programs of the 1960s, enacted during a time of confidence in the American economy, were expansive. They required a huge bureaucracy of federal employees to administer them. Because these programs were so popular with the public, the three presidential administrations of the 1970s found it very hard to end them. By 1980, social spending consumed 48 percent of the federal government's total spending. In a period of economic downturn, the government continued to spend money at a level appropriate to a more prosperous time.

Just as consumer debts do, the national debt accumulates interest. In 1970, the interest on the national, or public, debt was just under $20 billion. By the end of the decade, it had tripled to nearly $60 million. The decade also saw a rise in the difference between those people who had money and those who did not. Those who worked saw their wages increase as the 1970s wore on. Eager to spend their money, they did so quickly, and manufacturers could not keep up with demand. Since the demand for goods was greater than the supply of goods, the prices of those goods rose, and they did so at the fastest rate in history.

Those who did not work in the 1970s saw their ranks swell. In 1970, 3.2 million people were unemployed. A decade later, that number rose to 6.7 million. As unemployment rose, so did the welfare rolls (the number of people collecting welfare payments) and welfare expense. When the federal government needed more money to pay for that expense, it simply printed it. The additional currency increased the available money supply and diluted the value of the money already in circulation. At the beginning of the decade, the public held $49 billion in circulating currency. By 1980, the money supply exceeded $115 billion.

A major effect of this circumstance, an increased supply of money in circulation without saleable goods to balance that supply, was inflation. As prices went up, the value of a dollar did not keep up: One 1970 dollar could purchase only 43 cents' worth of goods in 1980. Although workers' average wages more than tripled during the decade, their dollars were worth less than half as much as when the decade began.

While the economy was faltering, so were U.S. businesses. Given the high relative price of American-made goods, consumers turned instead to lower-priced imported goods. The American electronics, automobile, and steel industries were especially hard hit. Moreover, the dollar had lost its value in foreign markets due to inflation, so American-made products did not sell well overseas. As a result, U.S. business production stagnated, or leveled off.

This combination of inflation in the economy and stagnation in production was called stagflation, and there was no painless remedy for it. The traditional cure for inflation, raising interest rates to force consumers to spend less money, would increase business stagnation. The cure for stagnation, having people spend more money to buy more products, would increase inflation.

President Nixon's plan to curb rising inflation rates included a ninety-day freeze on wages, prices, and rents. Set in motion in 1971, the president's plan worked in the short term, but the OPEC oil embargo of 1973–74 created shortages and pushed prices upward. Even after the embargo ended, prices remained high, fueling inflation and causing

Amtrak

After World War II (1939–45), passenger trains in the United States began to lose ground to the airplane and the private automobile. By the 1960s, very few people in the country relied on trains as a means of travel. To revive the dying rail industry, the U.S. Congress passed the Rail Passenger Service Act in October 1970. The act created the National Railroad Passenger Corporation, a private company better known as Amtrak (a combination of "America" and "track").

On May 1, 1971, the first Amtrak passenger train rode the rails, departing New York's Penn Station bound for Philadelphia. At its beginning, Amtrak employed just twenty-five people and operated an aging fleet of rail equipment, many trains without heating and air-conditioning systems. Despite this, the trains serviced 314 destinations, carrying 1,239,402 passengers per month in the first year of operation. Amtrak took over the passenger service of all but three rail companies in the country (it would take over these within the following decade).

In 1975, Amtrak began acquiring new locomotives and passenger lines. Steadily, it increased its service area, eventually operating over more than twenty-two thousand miles in forty-six states by the end of the twentieth century. While Amtrak has been successful in retaining nationwide passenger rail service, it has had a difficult time earning a profit outside the densely populated Northeast. Without continued financial support from the federal government, Amtrak's rail service would come to a halt.

unemployment rates to rise. Not wanting to impose burdensome federal regulations, President Carter tried to convince labor and industry to work together to fight inflation by voluntarily limiting wage and price increases. They refused. The president's other actions failed as well, and the decade ended with inflation and unemployment creeping ever higher.

WOMEN AND MINORITIES IN THE WORKPLACE

In the stagflation economy of the 1970s, women and minority workers increased their numbers in the workplace and made a few small gains in employment equality. Unfortunately, those gains had to be brought

The Rise of Compact Cars

In the wake of the oil embargo by the Organization of Petroleum Exporting Countries (OPEC) in 1973, severe oil and gasoline shortages arose in the United States. Suddenly Americans found themselves in long lines at gas pumps. Frustrated, drivers vented their anger on service-station attendants and on each other, fighting, stealing, and threatening violence. Some states closed gas stations on Sundays to discourage driving, while others instituted rationing programs. Overnight, it seemed, Americans wanted their automobiles to be small and energy efficient.

Refusing to continue purchasing the gas-guzzling behemoths produced by American automobile makers, consumers turned instead to small, fuel-efficient foreign cars manufactured in Germany, Sweden, and Japan. In response, Ford, Chrysler, and General Motors closed large-car plants and retooled to manufacture smaller compact cars to compete against the imports.

By 1974, compact-car sales surpassed those of standard large cars, and imported cars became increasingly popular. Volkswagen, Toyota, Saab, and Volvo automobiles were considered not only more economical and efficient but also superior to downsized American products such as the American Motors Gremlin, the Ford Pinto, or the Chevrolet Vega. The dominance of foreign compacts over their American counterparts would continue for some years.

about through laws and court actions. American business, dominated by white males before the 1970s largely because of cultural values, was slow to change, even when directed by the law to do so.

During World War II (1939–45), the war effort in America required women to enter the workforce in unprecedented numbers. Having experienced the working life, many female workers in the years after the war were unwilling to turn over their jobs to returning soldiers and other males and revert to a life at home. At the same time, the social upheavals of the 1950s and 1960s provided African Americans and other racial minorities with new rights in education and the workplace. Legislation and judicial order promised "equal opportunity," a phrase that resonated throughout the decades after World War II. While equal opportunity was

1975: Average wages and cost of goods

Median household income	$11,800.00
Minimum wage	$2.10
Cost of an average new home	$42,600.00
Cost of a gallon of regular gas	$0.57
Cost of a first-class stamp	$0.10
Cost of a gallon of milk	$1.57
Cost of a dozen eggs	$0.77
Cost of a loaf of bread	$0.33

a concept originally intended to correct racial injustice, the resulting laws frequently applied to gender as well as racial discrimination. Women and minorities saw hope in the phrase; employers saw only repressive regulation.

The key piece of legislation promoting racial and gender equality was the Civil Rights Act of 1964. It prohibited discrimination on the basis of race, color, religion, national origin, and, particularly in matters of employment, gender. Under this act, every business in the country that employed twenty-five people or more had to provide equal rights for employment and equal opportunity for promotion. Although the act was signed in the mid-1960s, it would take businesses years (and many more court actions) to obey it.

In 1970, women made up 38 percent of the civilian workforce. That same year, the U.S. Department of Labor issued guidelines to employers outlining measures to avoid gender discrimination. Seemingly disregarding the Civil Rights Act, passed just six years before, the guidelines applied only to companies with more than fifty employees. The following year, the U.S. Supreme Court ruled that businesses could not discriminate in hiring women with children unless similar restrictions were enforced against men. The Court also ruled that pension funds must be applied equally to both men and women. In 1972, the U.S. Senate passed the Equal Rights Amendment (ERA), a constitutional statement of equality between the sexes, but the amendment was never approved by three-quarters of the states, the number needed for adoption.

At the end of the decade, women made up 42.5 percent of the civilian workforce, a gain of just over 4 percent in ten years. But they earned substantially less than men doing similar jobs. As a group, women workers earned two-thirds as much money as white men and only slightly more than African American men.

While some business observers noted that blacks made some gains in the workplace, many African American political leaders described the 1970s as a wasted decade in terms of minority rights. The focus of the debate about racial discrimination during the 1970s was affirmative action (the policy of correcting injustices of the past by requiring that minorities be given preferential treatment in employment and promotion). The Equal Employment Opportunity Commission (EEOC), a federal government agency created by the 1964 Civil Rights Act, was responsible for pursuing affirmative-action remedies throughout the decade. However, only companies employing over one hundred workers were subject to EEOC authority, and most nongovernmental agencies were able to remove themselves from that authority completely.

In its highly publicized 1978 decision in the *Regents of the University of California* v. *Bakke* case, the U.S. Supreme Court supported the notion of affirmative action, but rejected the notion of quotas or setting aside a specific number of positions or places for certain individuals such as minorities. Yet, the following year, the Court held that well-paying jobs could be held for minorities.

By the end the 1970s, only white women increased their numbers in the workplace. The numbers of white men and black women decreased a few percentage points, probably due to rising unemployment. Of the four groups, black men fared the worst, their numbers dropping almost 8 percent. The most alarming statistic, though, was that 31.8 percent of the African American labor force between the ages of 16 and 24 was unemployed in 1980.

APPLE AND MICROSOFT: THE BEGINNING OF THE PERSONAL COMPUTER ERA

In January 1975, *Popular Electronics* magazine advertised the Altair 8800, a microcomputer kit manufactured by a company called MITS (Micro Instrumentation and Telemetry Systems). The Altair 8800 was a basic electronic gadget that had no video screen or keyboard. It was powered by an 8008 processing chip, with 256 bytes of random-access memory (RAM), enough to store only a small amount of information. By flipping a series of twenty-three switches, the user could input data to the processor. Responses came in the flashes of thirty-two lights on the front panel. It was a simple machine understandable only to specialists, but to Steven Jobs and Steve Wozniak, it represented the possibility of creating their own personal computer.

The two friends from California had been immersed in electronics for years. Wozniak was the true electronics wizard; Jobs was the dreamer whose genius lay in impressing his visions upon people. For a time in the early 1970s, the pair had sold "blue boxes" (built by Wozniak), pocket-size telephone attachments that allowed users to make free long-distance telephone calls illegally.

Apple president John Sculley (middle) with founders Steve Jobs and Steve Wozniak. ***Reproduced by permission of the Corbis Corporation.***

To realize their dream, the pair formed Apple Computer in early 1976. Some believe the name was in reference to the Beatles's record label, while others say it alluded to the time Jobs spent working on an apple orchard in Oregon. The company had only one product, the Apple I, which was little more than a circuit-board layout designed by Wozniak and manufactured in Jobs's garage. Buyers had to hook the computer up to a teletype or a television for a display, and input was accomplished by flipping switches. The processor made by Motorola had eight kilobytes of memory, making it more powerful than the early Altair. Although the pair made money on the Apple I, computer hobbyists did not take the product seriously, so Jobs developed a grander vision.

Integrating the ideas of several of his associates, he imagined a complete computing unit, consisting of a keyboard for input, a central processing unit for calculation, and a video screen for display. Wozniak had the intelligence to design such a unit; Jobs had the drive and persistence to inspire the work and design the packaging. When Wozniak's Apple II was introduced at the West Coast Computer Fair in April 1977, it was the hit of the show. No other computer could match its power or its integration of components.

Wozniak then expanded the minicomputer market enormously when he engineered a disk drive that allowed small computers to read and store large amounts of data from an outside source. The disk drive allowed users to save their work easily, and it allowed independent programmers to produce programs for the Apple. When VisiCalc, a small software producer, introduced its spreadsheet program for the Apple in January 1979 and a word-processing program called AppleWriter hit the market a few months later, the computer became useful to nonprogrammers for the first time. People quickly bought both the computers and the programs that made them work. By late 1979, Apple had sold fifty thousand computers, and both Jobs and Wozniak were millionaires.

Meanwhile, in Seattle, Washington, in the early 1970s, a teenager named William Henry Gates was demonstrating a remarkable ability to understand computer logic and turn it to practical uses. When the Altair 8800 was introduced, Gates was studying applied mathematics at Harvard University. He and his friend Paul Allen quickly saw a way to make the machine useful: They would write a version of BASIC for the machine, and it could then be used for practical computations. The conviction that computers were made useful by such programs—software—was the central principle that guided Gates's and Allen's efforts.

BASIC was a simplified language that turned computer programmers' instructions into information the machine could understand. Using BASIC, a programmer could instruct a machine to add two numbers, for example, and BASIC turned those instructions into electronic codes that caused the machine to perform its calculation. But each different kind of processing chip had a different set of electronic codes, so BASIC had to be adapted for each of them. Gates and Allen wrote the first and best adaptation of BASIC for the 8008 chip the Altair used, and it was the basis of their success. They sold their BASIC to MITS and started a new company that specialized in writing versions of BASIC and other languages for different types of computers.

The business aim of Micro-Soft, as the company name was then written (it briefly became MicroSoft before taking its present form of Microsoft), was to provide programs exclusively for computer manufacturers and demand a flat-fee payment in advance. In the early years, Gates, Allen, and their colleagues adapted BASIC for various hardware configurations, enhancing their programs as they went along. They also provided versions of other standard programming languages such as Common Business-Oriented Language (COBOL) and Formula Translation (FORTRAN) for use on the burgeoning number of small computers being introduced. In 1977, Gates dropped out of Harvard after his junior year and moved the Microsoft office to the Seattle area. That same year, General Electric tapped Gates and Allen to provide BASIC for use in its computers. In 1978, with sales of more than $1.3 million, Microsoft made its first deal in Japan, providing software for NEC, a computer company that dominated the Japanese market.

By 1979, companies were selling personal computing machines were being sold that had screens, keyboards, and, most important, disk drives that could store programs and save any data the programs generated. But each type of computer required a customized version of software tailored to its hardware configuration. As a result, unless a user knew BASIC or another programming language or was content with the limited number of programs available for that particular computer, the machine would not do much.

Gates and Allen began attacking the problem of developing a software operating system that would serve to translate standard programs for various machines. By the end of 1979, they were marketing stand-alone BASIC, an adaptation of their master version that could, with minimal user programming, run on most standard computers. They had taken the first step toward developing an industry-standard operating system that would allow various software to be used on a variety of machines.

For More Information

BOOKS

Cole, Dermot. *Amazing Pipeline Stories: How Building the Trans-Alaska Pipeline Transformed Life in America's Last Frontier.* Kenmore, WA: Epicenter Press, 1997.

Linzmayer, Owen W. *Apple Confidential: The Real Story of Apple Computer, Inc.* San Francisco: No Starch Press, 1999.

Manes, Stephen, and Paul Andrews. *Gates: How Microsoft's Mogul Reinvented an Industry-and Made Himself the Richest Man in America.* New York: Doubleday, 1993.

Strasser, J. B., and Laurie Becklund. *Swoosh: The Unauthorized Story of Nike and the Men Who Played There.* San Diego: Harcourt Brace Jovanovich, 1992.

WEB SITES

Civil Rights Center (CRC) Home Page. http://www.dol.gov/dol/oasam/crchome.htm (accessed on February 26, 2002).

Nobel e-Museum. http://www.nobel.se/index.html (accessed on February 26, 2002).

U.S. Department of Labor Home Page. http://www.dol.gov/ (accessed on February 26, 2002).

U.S. Equal Employment Opportunity Commission Home Page. http://www.eeoc.gov/ (accessed on February 26, 2002).

chapter three

Education

1970: **February 8** At a Birmingham rally, former Alabama governor George Wallace urges southern governors to defy federal education integration orders.

1970: **May 4** Four students are killed and eight wounded at Kent State University in Ohio by National Guard troops at a rally protesting the Vietnam War.

1971: Census data shows the proportion of Americans with high-school diplomas has risen from 38 percent in the 1940s to 75 percent.

1971: African Americans, who make up 11 percent of the total U.S. population, represent just 7 percent of the college population.

1971: **April 20** The U.S. Supreme Court unanimously rules that busing to achieve racial balance is constitutional in cases where local officials permitted segregation to occur.

1972: **January 18** Sixteen African American protestors interrupt an examination in a Stanford University course taught by Nobel Prize-winning physicist William Shockley to object to his allegedly racist theories.

1972: **March 18** Twenty-nine men and women draw lots and begin living together in a University of Michigan housing unit to "break down some of the barriers between the sexes."

1972: **March 19** The U.S. Supreme Court rules that state colleges and universities cannot expel a student for campus distribution of material that administrators deem offensive.

1973: **April 4** The U.S. District Court in Atlanta orders a compromise school integration plan.

1973: **September 11** Eight hundred thousand students nationwide are unable to return to school because of teacher strikes.

1973: **November 13** The U.S. Department of Health, Education, and Welfare rejects college desegregation plans filed by state systems in Arkansas, Florida, Georgia, Louisiana, Mississippi, North Carolina, Oklahoma, Pennsylvania, and Virginia.

1974: **January 17** The U.S. Department of Health, Education, and Welfare says racial discrimination still exists in the schools in Topeka, Kansas, the site of the landmark 1954 educational desegregation lawsuit *Brown* v. *Board of Education of Topeka.*

1974: **January 21** The U.S. Supreme Court rules unanimously that a San Francisco school district must provide English-language instruction for Chinese students.

1974: June Federal judge Arthur Garrity rules that the Boston School Committee has deliberately segregated schools by race; he orders a plan exchanging students between white South Boston and black Roxbury school districts.

1974: September 14 White mobs in Boston shout racist remarks to buses carrying African Americans to their schools. Violence ensues. A month later, Massachusetts governor Francis Sargent calls out the National Guard to restore order in South Boston.

1975: January 5 The Educational Testing Service reports women with doctorates are discriminated against in matters of salary and promotions in higher education.

1975: February 25 The U.S. Supreme Court rules that school-board members are liable for damages if students prove their rights were denied.

1976: January 26 Court-ordered busing in Detroit begins without incident.

1976: February 24 Federal judge Arthur Garrity imposes a 20 percent quota for black administrators in the Boston school system.

1977: January 17 A Boston Schools Department report asserts the quality of public education has deteriorated since the start of busing.

1977: April 19 The U.S. Supreme Court rules that school officials can spank students without violating their constitutional rights.

1978: February 21 The U.S. Supreme Court leaves standing a U.S. Circuit Court of Appeals decision that the University of Missouri cannot refuse to recognize Gay Liberation, a student homosexual group, as an official campus organization.

1978: April 7 New York City drops its 1977 plan of assigning teachers on the basis of race.

1978: June 28 The U.S. Supreme Court rules in favor of Allen Bakke, who was protesting as unconstitutional the special-admissions policy of the medical school at the University of California, Davis.

1979: June 11 The U.S. Supreme Court rules unanimously that federally funded colleges do not have to admit all handicapped applicants nor make extensive modifications to accommodate them.

1979: August 15 The Ann Arbor, Michigan, school board approves a program to teach "Black English" to all twenty-eight teachers at Martin Luther King Elementary.

1979: September 10 Cleveland, Ohio, schools desegregate, capping off a six-year court battle.

Overview

The 1970s was a decade of transformation in education. Efforts were made to increase opportunities and improve performance of previously disadvantaged minorities: African Americans, immigrants, the disabled, and, to a certain degree, women. Many of these efforts met with success. For example, more minority students attended formerly all-white schools and later gained greater entrance to higher education; more nonnative speakers of English received bilingual instruction; the disabled were granted new access to a free public education; and women broke down employment barriers at all levels of academia.

However, achievement by public-school students as a whole suffered. Every age group except primary-school students performed worse on standardized tests than in the previous decade. The most significant test-score declines were found among high-school students. This led many people to believe the nation was in the midst of an educational crisis.

A growing debate then arose between traditionalists and progressives on how best to educate American children. Traditionalists (sometimes called back-to-basics proponents) argued that students learn best when given lots of structure, specific standards of performance, and a heavy dose of memorization of key facts and concepts. On the other hand, progressives believed just as strongly that students need freedom and time to pursue questions that interest them, and that sometimes structure hinders student learning. In the early 1970s, more and more schools began to pursue a progressive approach to learning. By mid-decade, however, in response to parents' concerns about low test scores, many schools moved back toward a more traditional approach.

American schools in the 1970s reflected the economic, racial, and social problems in the country as a whole. The major political issue regarding education in the decade was the attempt to eliminate segregation (the practice of keeping ethnic or racial groups separate). During the late 1960s and early 1970s, great strides had been made in the South, where federal rulings banning segregation forced schools to accommodate minority students. The combined power of the courts and the threatened loss of essential federal funds brought the battles over segregation in the South to a halt. In 1974, a U.S. Department of Health, Education, and Welfare report showed that by a wide margin, schools in the South were the most integrated in the nation. However, that same report showed that schools in the Northeast were more segregated than they had been in 1970.

In the Northeast, the Midwest and the West, many children still attended schools that were highly segregated due to the location of school district lines. Especially in large cities, where public housing was clustered in downtown areas, minority students tended to populate inner-city schools, whereas white students attended more affluent suburban schools. Usually, these schools were administered by separate school districts. To eliminate this inherent segregation, the courts issued orders to bus students across district lines, black students to white schools and white students to black schools. Many parents and politicians complained loudly about the policy of busing as a means to end segregation. In Boston, serious resistance resulted in rioting and the Massachusetts National Guard had to restore order. By decade's end, many busing programs had been abandoned.

Allan Bakke (1940–) In 1972, Allan Bakke applied for admission to eleven medical schools in the country, including the University of California, Davis, his first choice. All eleven schools rejected Bakke, despite his high entrance exam scores. Because his scores were better than some minority applicants who gained admission to the University of California, Bakke sued the university for discrimination. The U.S. Supreme Court ruled in 1978 that while the school could act to diversify its student body, it could not set aside a specific number of places for minorities. Admitted that fall, Bakke graduated in 1982. ***Photo reproduced by permission of the Corbis Corporation.***

Benjamin S. Bloom (1913–) Education professor Benjamin S. Bloom aimed to remake education into a more scientific activity. His organized approach to teaching was welcomed by those in education opposed to the open or free concept of learning popular during the 1970s. In *Handbook on Formative and Summative Evaluation of Student Learning,* published in 1971, Bloom outlined how educational objectives should be formulated and tested in all subject areas. When steadily falling student test scores became a hallmark of the decade, Bloom's orderly approach to teaching was quickly adopted by many as a possible cure.

Jonathan Kozol (1936–) Jonathan Kozol used his experiences as a teacher to become an outspoken education critic. His prominence in the world of educational criticism had begun in 1967, when he published *Death at an Early Age.* This day-to-day account of life for teachers and students in a ghetto school received a National Book Award. Throughout the 1970s, he published many other books about ghetto schools, illiteracy, and the effects of a segregated education on children. These highly influential books were studied by the general public as well as by professional educators. ***Photo reproduced by permission of AP/Wide World Photos.***

Charles E. Silberman (1925–) In 1970, journalist Charles E. Silberman published *Crisis in the Classroom,* a critique of U.S. education that seized the attention of almost everyone in the country. Among his recommendations to overhaul education, Silberman thought American elementary schools should be modeled on English ones, where the activities of the students were determined, to a great extent, by their interests and needs, not those of the teacher. His work set the stage for many public debates about educational improvement. Reformers cited his criticisms and recommendations throughout the decade.

DESEGREGATION AND BUSING

At the beginning of the 1970s, busing students to public schools was common, with about 43 percent of the nation's schoolchildren riding buses each day. Busing children from school to school in order to provide school districts with racial balance, however, was new. Busing for large-scale desegregation (the elimination of separation of the races) began in 1971, when the U.S. Supreme Court decided that many school districts had not complied with the 1954 *Brown* v. *Board of Education of Topeka* decision. In that court case, the justices had ruled that segregation in public schools was "inherently unequal." In a decision the following year, the Court had ordered desegregation "with all deliberate speed."

After the decision, however, most students stayed where they were, and thus most school districts remained segregated. Eventually, in 1971, in *Swann* v. *Charlotte-Mecklenburg Board of Education*, the Court decided that "all deliberate speed" had not been speedy enough, ordering the Charlotte, North Carolina, school district to bus its students across district lines to achieve desegregation. The justices reasoned that busing was warranted because the district had deliberately and knowingly taken steps to prevent integration of their public schools.

During the 1970s, court orders supporting busing were handed down all over the United States. When those decisions were appealed to the U.S. Supreme Court, the Court often upheld the argument to use busing to eliminate segregation. In 1974, however, in the *Milliken* v. *Bradley* decision, the Supreme Court struck down a district-court ruling that required busing between Detroit's black schools and suburban white schools. The majority of the justices reasoned that the suburban districts were not engaging in segregation according to the law, and thus no busing remedy was necessary. Yet, a year later, the same Supreme Court ruled just the opposite in Delaware, ordering busing to mix white suburban schools of New Castle County with those of Wilmington, which were 85 percent black.

Throughout the decade, American courts ordered mandatory busing in several cities, despite the likelihood that those school districts' segregation might have been an unintentional result of housing patterns. In some urban areas, policies of the Federal Housing Authority and the Veterans' Administration had produced segregated neighborhoods. Examples included Louisville, Cleveland, Los Angeles, and Indianapolis, where black students from the cities were bused to white suburban schools.

As police stand guard, black students arrive at the predominately white South Boston High School where thousands of white Boston students refused to enter court-ordered desegregated schools on the first day of classes in 1974. **Photo reproduced by permission of the Corbis Corporation.**

These policies were soon followed by objections from parents to programs that attempted to go beyond forbidding discrimination. Supporters of busing argued that these measures were necessary to compensate African Americans and other minorities for generations of segregation. Debates were long and loud. In 1974 in Boston, the court-ordered busing was disrupted by violence and a boycott by white students. South Boston High School was eventually put under federal management because of neighborhood resistance to busing.

While the success of court-ordered busing was not clear, the cost of the plans was. Two years of forced busing cost Boston more than $56 million. In five months, Detroit spent eleven million dollars on busing, excluding police costs. Even more startling was public opposition to busing, which was overwhelming. In 1972, a Harris survey found that 73 percent of the public was opposed to busing; only 20 percent favored it. Blacks and whites equally disliked it. In 1975, a federal government study found that busing to achieve desegregation had little impact on academic achievement: In school districts where busing took place, the scores of white students did not drop, while the scores of African American students rose only slightly.

OPPOSITE PAGE Hispanic American students in a bilingual classroom in Texas. **Photograph by Curtis Dowall. Reproduced by permission of the Texas Catholic Herald.**

BILINGUAL EDUCATION: A GROWING CONTROVERSY

During the 1970s, twenty states enacted local bilingual-education acts, signaling a major shift in educational policy. Prior to 1968, many states had approved legislation requiring that all teaching in public schools be conducted in English. In seven of those states, teachers had formerly faced criminal penalties for leading bilingual classes. That all changed in 1968 when the U.S. Congress passed the Bilingual Education Act as Title VII of the revised Elementary and Secondary Education Act (ESEA).

Equal Access for the Disabled

The Vocational Rehabilitation Act of 1973 triggered a major transformation of federal policy in public education. It stated that "No handicapped individual shall be excluded from any program or activity receiving federal financial assistance." At this time, it was estimated that 62 percent of the intellectually and emotionally disabled students in the United States were not receiving public education. Since every school district in the country was receiving some federal funding, the implications were enormous for the public schools. In 1975, in order to clarify the schools' responsibilities, the U.S. Congress passed what became known as the Education for All Handicapped Children Act. It guaranteed all disabled students a right to a free public education. The act applied to all children ages three through twenty-one who were physically handicapped, deaf, blind, learning disabled, or emotionally disturbed. The act suggested that, when possible, these students should be educated alongside mainstream students.

The states were forced to provide this free education, and the federal government provided only a modest amount of the necessary funding. States also had to find, train, and hire special education teachers. Often, traditionally trained teachers with no background in special education found themselves dealing with children with special needs. Local agencies struggled to provide extra funding to help in the education of the many children who previously had not attended public schools. Despite such efforts, by the end of the decade, many school administrators frequently found themselves in court dealing with parents who challenged school decisions regarding their disabled children.

To meet the growing demand for bilingual education, it was estimated that twenty-four thousand bilingual teachers would be needed by the end of the 1970s. Since only nineteen hundred bilingual teachers were entering the field each year, however, many school districts continued to struggle to provide bilingual instruction. Because of this, many lawsuits on behalf of Chinese and Hispanic students were filed, and courts ruled in their favor. In 1974, the U.S. Congress revised the ESEA, providing further funding for the training of bilingual teachers.

Yet, by mid-decade, questions began to arise about the worth of some bilingual education programs, especially those for Hispanic students. The U.S. Office of Education (USOE) reported in 1976 that serious shortcomings existed in thirty-eight programs investigated by project directors. Students were staying in all-day bilingual programs long after they were able to participate in English-speaking classes. These findings caused the USOE to tighten regulations for bilingual programs so that only students who were significantly limited in English were admitted.

That same year, a study by the American Institute for Research found that Hispanics in regular classes did about as well in general subjects as those in bilingual programs; students in bilingual programs did slightly better in math, but slightly worse in English classes. By 1979, when the annual cost of the federal bilingual program had risen to $150 million (a twenty-fold increase over a decade before), attacks began to mount. Some education critics claimed that, in addition to keeping students beyond the basic preparation for English-language classes, extended dual-language programs threatened the "melting pot" function of American public schools.

THE LITERACY CRISIS

The debate over the literacy and basic academic skills of American students began in the early 1970s and heated to the boiling point by the middle of the decade. At the end of 1975, *Newsweek* magazine ran an alarming cover story on the perceived decline in American education, alerting the country to the possibility that American schools were graduating students who could not even write a comprehensible sentence in English.

That year, the SAT scores of U.S. students had declined to their lowest point in twelve years. (The SAT is a standardized test administered to high school students by the College Board and required for admission by many U.S. colleges. The test is designed to estimate how students are likely to succeed in college.) Concern about falling test scores also had been mounting inside the nation's capital. The National Institute of Education held a special conference on the decline, but the researchers who met in Washington, D.C., in June 1975 could not reach a consensus on what the lower scores meant. Their report, which claimed that the test scores did not represent a general collapse in literacy, cast doubt about what the SAT measured and whether it accurately reflected student skills.

Because of the importance of the SAT to many of the nation's best universities, public attention was focused on the question of whether the test takers or the test makers were to blame for the problem. There was also great confusion on the part of the public as to what the SAT actually measured. Its creators defined the SAT as an aptitude test designed to measure natural abilities. Cramming for the exam would

U.S. High School Dropout Percentage: 1975

Total, all races	13.9
Total, white	11.4
Total, black	22.9
Total, Hispanic	29.2
Male, all races	13.3
Male, white	11.0
Male, black	23.0
Male, Hispanic	26.7
Female, all races	14.5
Female, white	11.8
Female, black	22.9
Female, Hispanic	31.6

therefore do no good. Many educators who believed in a traditional classroom approach declared the SAT an achievement test: Declining scores on it, they said, was obvious evidence that students were not achieving and could not write, even though test takers did not have to write an essay during the exam.

Nearly everyone from parents to researchers suggested causes for the decline in test scores and for the possible corresponding decline in literacy. Many conservatives who promoted a traditional approach to education—studying reading, writing, and arithmetic—were convinced that schooling innovations during the 1960s and early 1970s had been at fault. They argued that liberal education—too little reading and writing, too many "soft" electives, and too few required academic courses—was the culprit. Even though the vast majority of public schools were still traditional in nature in the 1970s, some liberals agreed that the activism of the 1960s that had filtered down to high schools had an anti-intellectual bias. Others blamed the decline in test scores on too much television and an unstable family life. Most testing experts suspected another explanation: that more people from nontraditional, nonacademic backgrounds were applying to college in greater numbers. The SAT was therefore no longer testing an elite scholarly group.

Watching American History

Public television made an extraordinary appearance in America's classrooms in 1976. At more than three hundred colleges and universities, students took courses based on thirteen episodes of a television series called *The Adams Family Chronicles*. This Public Broadcasting Service (PBS) show analyzed the influential family who helped create the United States of America. Featured members of the Massachusetts family included John Adams, America's second president, his wife Abigail, and their son John Quincy Adams, the sixth president. Although for two decades television had been used sporadically in the classroom, this exemplary series became the centerpiece of many courses, not merely an aid to instruction. Many professors throughout the country hailed the series, believing it captured the attention of students as no lecture or book ever could.

Regardless of the causes of the SAT decline, the phenomenon set off a wave of new standardized testing procedures around 1977. During that year, twenty-nine states moved toward competency-based skill programs, with minimum achievement goals tested from grade to grade. Eventually, two-thirds of the states adopted such plans. To fix the literacy crisis, politicians and parents demanded that more and harder skills be tested in the nation's schools.

TEXTBOOKS UNDER FIRE

Mel and Norma Gabler of Hawkins, Texas, began a crusade for textbook censorship in 1961 when their son brought home a history text the Gablers believed was filled with anti-American and anti-Christian views. The couple soon ignited a firestorm of national criticism of educational publishing companies. At its height in the mid-1970s, this protest affected the textbook selection process throughout the United States. Most of the serious debates, however, were concentrated in the twenty-two states (mostly in the South and Southwest) where textbooks had to be approved by state, rather than local, authorities.

To the Gablers and their supporters, modern textbooks questioned and undermined traditional religious values, and they easily swayed the minds of young Americans. In 1972, testifying before the Texas Textbook

Committee, Norma Gabler objected to one chapter in *Search for Freedom*, a fifth-grade U.S. history text published by Macmillan. Gabler believed the book was irreligious, equating Cesar Chavez, Martin Luther King Jr., and Mohandas Gandhi with Jesus of Nazareth. She furthermore objected that the text devoted $^{6}/_{12}$ pages to actress Marilyn Monroe while it barely discussed U.S. president George Washington.

Gabler's appearance and testimony gained instantaneous media attention and landed her on the front page of many U.S. newspapers. Thousands of new followers joined her and her husband's cause, forcing textbook publishers into costly revisions of their books. After these successes, the Gablers went on to challenge school curricula in reading, writing, math, biology, psychology, and sociology courses. They believed only traditional approaches to education should be followed. They also thought writing programs that emphasized self-expression and imagination over grammatical correctness eroded standards of language usage. They attacked new approaches in the teaching of mathematics, suggesting they destroyed a students' beliefs in anything absolute. Finally, the Gablers and their supporters examined biology, psychology, and sociology courses for what they considered to be objectionable discussions of homosexuality and sexually deviant behavior. They succeeded in restricting open discussion of these topics and eliminating whole sections of textbooks that addressed such issues.

The movement inspired by the Gablers peaked in 1974 in West Virginia when Alice Moore, a first-term member of the Kanawha County Board of Education, challenged texts she believed attacked basic social values. After extensive media coverage, supporters of Moore protested by keeping home more than ten thousand of their children on the first day of school. The next day, thirty-five hundred miners launched a strike in sympathy with the protest movement. Exchanges of gunfire occurred around schools. Cars, homes, and schools were firebombed. Eight thousand protesters marched in Charleston, the state capital. After investigating the controversy, however, National Education Association officials concluded that allowing the protesters to change textbook and curriculum guidelines would be allowing one group to impose its set of values upon the students in the entire area.

The conservative scrutiny of textbooks inspired liberals, especially within academia, to conduct their own review of textbooks. Contrary to the Gablers, many argued that textbooks were biased toward conservative interests, especially in their wholehearted approval of American business and industry. Although federal officials called on textbook publishers to consider different approaches, the debate over school texts and curricula continued throughout the 1970s.

The Death of New Math

At the beginning of the 1970s, big textbook companies began to publish math materials based almost exclusively on the curricular movement known as "new math." Creators of the new-math approach opposed the idea that the main object of mathematics instruction was arithmetic proficiency. New math put theory before practice. Students were exposed to sophisticated concepts such as set theory, number theory, and symbolic logic. The belief was that if theory came before practice, all math reasoning would fall into place, including computation. This purely intellectual approach was touted as being more fun than memorizing arithmetic rules. With the recent development of hand-held calculators, many mathematics professors argued that students would not need to know how to perform basic addition, subtraction, division, and multiplication calculations.

California schools had led the way in adopting the new-math programs. However, when students' scores dropped 20 percent on standardized math tests in the state in 1973, parents and many teachers began to complain about the new-math approach. All over the state the results were the same: Students who had good math skills when they entered the program did worse afterward. Not surprisingly, teachers all over the country reported frustrations. Many teachers were not only intellectually unprepared for the change but also resistant to the entire philosophy. The hurriedly compiled textbooks contributed to the problems. In 1973 McGraw-Hill, one of the nation's leading textbook publishers, discontinued its new-math texts. Soon all the other companies followed and, without prepared texts, the movement died rapidly

EDUCATIONAL PROGRESS FOR WOMEN: TITLE IX AND BEYOND

In the 1970s, women in education were beginning to organize for change. They sought to establish female role models in leadership positions and gender equality at all levels of the education community. These efforts ranged from eliminating gender bias from elementary-school textbooks to increasing the numbers of women faculty members in higher education. More important, the movement hoped to emphasize the necessity for a woman to be educated so as to increase the options available to her in life.

Previously, women were all but absent from the curriculum of secondary schools and colleges. However, during the 1970s, this changed dramatically. By decade's end, hundreds of courses and programs in women's studies had been established in higher education. As early as 1974, 4,990 courses in women's studies were taught at 995 institutions of higher learning. By 1979, the number of programs on campuses had tripled, with some large programs offering from seventy-five to one hundred courses annually.

The curricula in most women's studies programs were based on teaching students, both men and women, to understand issues such as women in history, the history and function of the family, women in the workforce and the economy, laws affecting women, and the history of women in social movements. By the end of the decade, nearly every campus offered one or more courses in which women wrote the texts, taught the courses, and offered previously ignored perspectives on traditional subject matter.

Another milestone for women in education was Title IX of the Educational Amendments Act of 1972. Intended to guarantee young women

Title IX not only guaranteed young women equal access to more educational programs, but it also opened up many more organized sports programs to girls. ***Photograph by Geoffrey Bluh.***

Major of the Decade

Reflecting American society, the mood on American campuses became more spiritual and introspective in the 1970s. As a result, courses in psychology became more popular. By mid-decade, nearly every psychology department in the nation was flooded with students pursuing the "in" major. Nationally, enrollment in psychology graduate studies was up 114 percent compared to five years earlier. Many advisers saw this trend as the expression of a new attitude among college students: After a decade of protesting social problems, students now became preoccupied with the individual and his or her inner problems. In addition, many students became involved with transcendental meditation, encounter groups, and other searches for self-understanding.

Students who finished psychology graduate programs were also researching different types of psychological questions from those of the 1960s. Experts in psychology tackled problems not in the lab but in the real world. They studied the effects on people of such problems as pollution, drugs, alcohol abuse, crime, and sexual dysfunction. The demand for psychology professors rose from twenty-five hundred in 1970 to seven thousand in 1973, and no real job glut appeared in this field until the end of the decade.

equal access to any educational program funded by the federal government, it did far more. In a 1978 study by the U.S. Department of Health, Education, and Welfare of ten major universities and their compliance with Title IX, it was reported that every university in the study had upgraded women's athletic programs. In addition, those colleges with the biggest, most successful programs for men made the greatest efforts in creating strong programs for women.

Two other statutes went beyond Title IX to improve educational opportunities for women: The Women's Equity Act of 1974 provided funds to universities to develop curricula and educational activities to improve programs in vocational and physical education for women. The Vocational Education Act of 1976 prohibited sexual discrimination and bias in any educational program, including vocational education. Due in part to the power of these acts and the organized women's movement, women made significant strides on all levels of education by the end of the 1970s.

MINORITIES, ADMISSIONS POLICIES, AND THE BAKKE DECISION

To assure equal opportunities to students who were economically or educationally disadvantaged, many universities and schools of higher learning established special minority-admissions programs during the 1970s. Even in schools that did not openly promote these types of programs, many admissions officers reserved the right to select students who would help create a diverse student body. Near the end of the decade, the U.S. Supreme Court examined these policies in the famous *Regents of the University of California* v. *Bakke* decision. Legal guidelines were then established that in many ways upheld special consideration for minority applicants.

When a new medical school opened at the Davis campus of the University of California system in 1968, the minority population of that state was 23 percent. Yet no African American, Mexican American or Native American student was admitted into the entering class (three Asian students were admitted). After 1971, however, a special-admissions program at the university set aside sixteen seats for students who could be considered economically or educationally disadvantaged. A check-off box was included on the admissions form for such students to identify themselves. Although race was not a stated consideration of the program, no white student was ever admitted under the program.

The program began to change the make-up of the university's medical-school class: Between 1970 and 1974, of the 452 students admitted, 27 were African American and 39 were Mexican American. Without the special-admissions program, only one African American student and six Mexican American students would have been accepted. Each applicant was assigned a benchmark score: a composite of his or her interview, grade-point ratio from undergraduate school, grade-point ratio of science courses, Medical Comprehensive Achievement Test (MCAT) score, letters of recommendation, and personal background. Each of these criteria was rated on a scale.

Allen Bakke, a white Vietnam veteran, applied to the medical school at the university in 1973. Out of a possible 500 benchmark score, Bakke received 468. No general-admissions applicant with a score under 470 was accepted in 1973, however, so Bakke reapplied in 1974. This time, he received a score of 549 out of a possible 600. Again, he was not admitted, even though applicants with lower scores were accepted in both years under the special-admissions program. Bakke then sued the university. He claimed he had been denied admission on the basis of race, a practice that violated Article I of the California Constitution, the Fourteenth Amendment of the U.S. Constitution, and Title VI of the Civil Rights Act of 1964.

Bakke's case went all the way to the U.S. Supreme Court. In June 1978, in *Regents of the University of California* v. *Bakke*, the Court ruled in favor of Bakke, striking down the university's admissions policy. The decision affected admissions policies nationwide. Even though the Court ordered the university to admit Bakke, it upheld the constitutionality of special minority admissions. In its decision, the Court maintained that only rigid quotas (the setting aside of a specific number of positions) for minority students were illegal, such as what the University of California, Davis, had done by setting aside sixteen places for minorities.

In the last two years of the decade, many graduate and professional schools changed their admissions policy to meet the *Bakke* guidelines. The rule for admissions was simple: no rigid quotas and no students barred from competing solely on the basis of race. Thus, the U.S. Supreme Court decision on Bakke's case was not a legal command to dismantle affirmative-action programs (those programs intended to counter discrimination against minorities and women). Instead, it prompted universities to develop more carefully conceived plans to encourage diversity without denying a place for any qualified student.

THE RISE OF BLACK STUDIES

Black activism on college campuses in the 1960s had been widespread. African American students demanded input into admissions policies and course offerings. Their tactics to achieve change were varied: Sometimes they worked through standard political channels, sometimes they protested peacefully, and sometimes they resorted to violent takeovers. These tactics worked. By the early 1970s, African American students and faculty had succeeded in achieving many reforms that had seemed out of reach just a decade earlier. Suddenly, universities were making long-term commitments to faculty recruited specifically to teach courses in black studies.

The essential aims of most black studies programs were similar: to help change the image of African Americans, to provide African Americans with a psychological identity, to foster racial understanding, and to present an organized study of black people and their accomplishments. Because so many universities were hiring professors to set up programs for black studies, there was a great demand for teacher training. Many campuses were somewhat alarmed at the speed with which programs were instituted. At Harvard, for example, a special faculty committee on African and African American studies labored to write a policy about the program while it was being developed. The committee hoped that the program would serve both black and white students, highlighting the history, literature, art, and music of African Americans while combating racism at the same time.

Once the new field began to be established, several black scholarly journals debuted. One of the first was the *Black Scholar,* which published its first issue in 1970. This journal provided a forum for black scholarship during the decade, regardless of the academic field of the writer. However, although it promised scholarship, its first issue featured articles by many nonscholars. Among them were black radical activists such as Stokely Carmichael, Bobby Seale, and Eldridge Cleaver, whose articles encouraged overthrowing the upper classes in America.

Many mainstream, predominantly white universities welcomed minority students. They built departments of black studies or at least offered courses such as black history or the sociology of minority groups. Recruitment was so successful that by 1976, two-thirds of the eight hundred thousand African American college students in the country were attending formerly white institutions. This shift in attendance trends left many of America's 120 historically black colleges and universities in jeopardy. Ironically, many black institutions found themselves pressured to admit white students in order to keep federal funding of certain grants intact. Some young African Americans, however, remained loyal to their historic schools, helping to keep the proud traditions of those schools alive.

For More Information

BOOKS

Banfield, Susan. *The Bakke Case: Quotas in College Admissions.* Berkeley Heights, NJ: Enslow, 1998.

Formisano, Ronald P. *Boston Against Busing: Race, Class, and Ethnicity in the 1960s and 1970s.* Chapel Hill: University of North Carolina Press, 1991

Kozol, Jonathon. *Death at an Early Age: The Destruction of the Hearts and Minds of Negro Children in the Boston Public Schools.* New York: New American Library, 1967.

Kozol, Jonathon. *Savage Inequalities: Children in America's Schools.* Reprint edition. New York: Harper Perennial, 1992.

Sheils, Merrill. "Why Johnny Can't Write." *Newsweek* (December 8, 1975): 58–65.

Silberman, Charles E. *Crisis in the Classroom: The Remaking of American Education.* New York: Random House, 1970.

WEB SITES

Affirmative Action History: Bakke and Beyond. http://www.infoplease.com/spot/affirmative1.html (accessed on March 12, 2002).

Education Week: Desegregation. http://www.edweek.org/context/topics/issuespage.cfm?id=27 (accessed on March 12, 2002).

National Center for Education Statistics Home Page. http://nces.ed.gov/ (accessed on March 12, 2002).

Title IX at 25. http://www.aauw.org/1000/title9bd.html (accessed March 12, 2002).

U.S. Department of Education. http://www.ed.gov/index.jsp (accessed on March 12, 2002).

chapter four Government, Politics, and Law

1970: February 20 U.S. Secretary of State Henry Kissinger begins secret talks in Paris with Le Duc Tho, representative of North Vietnam, focused on ending the Vietnam War.

1970: May 4 Members of the National Guard kill four students during an antiwar protest at Kent State University in Ohio.

1971: March 29 U.S. Army First Lieutenant William Calley is found guilty of murder in the 1968 massacre of Vietnamese civilians at My (pronounced MEE) Lai.

1971: June 10 President Richard M. Nixon ends the U.S. trade embargo of China.

1971: September 9 Prisoners riot at the Attica State Correctional Facility in Attica, New York. After four days, Governor Nelson Rockefeller orders state police to retake the prison by force.

1972: February 21 Nixon becomes the first American president to visit China.

1972: May 27 Nixon becomes the first American president to visit Moscow. While in the Soviet Union, he signs treaties relating to antiballistic missiles and other strategic weapons.

1972: June 17 Police arrest five men for breaking into the Democratic National Committee's headquarters at the Watergate office complex in Washington, D.C. Three of the men have ties to Nixon's reelection campaign.

1973: January 20 The U.S. Supreme Court rules in *Roe* v. *Wade* by a vote of six to three that women's privacy rights prevent states from prohibiting abortion in the first trimester of pregnancy.

1973: January 27 In Paris, Kissinger and Le Duc Tho sign the cease-fire agreement on Vietnam.

1973: June 25–29 Former White House counsel John Dean testifies before the Ervin congressional investigative committee, implicating himself, H.R. Haldeman, John Ehrlichman, John Mitchell, Nixon, and others in the Watergate cover-up.

1973: October 23 Eight resolutions to impeach Nixon are introduced in the U.S. House of Representatives.

1974: July 24 The U.S. Supreme Court unanimously rules that Nixon must turn over tapes requested by the special prosecutor. The Court holds that the president does not have unlimited "executive privilege" as he claims.

1974: **July 24** The House Judiciary Committee commences formal impeachment hearings against Nixon.

1974: **August 8** In a televised address, Nixon announces his resignation from the presidency, effective at noon on August 9. He becomes the first president in American history to resign.

1975: **April 29** The last Americans leave the U.S. embassy in Saigon, South Vietnam. General Duong Van Minh of the South Vietnamese army surrenders to the North Vietnamese the following day.

1976: **July 3–4** The nation celebrates the Bicentennial (two-hundredth anniversary of its independence) with festivals and political events around the country.

1976: **November 15** The United States vetoes the admission of Vietnam to the United Nations.

1977: **January 21** President Jimmy Carter signs an unconditional pardon for almost all Vietnam War-era draft evaders.

1977: **June 20** The U.S. Supreme Court upholds by a vote of six to three the authority of the states to refuse to pay for poor women's abortions unless a physician says that it is medically necessary.

1978: **September 17** President Carter, Prime Minister Menachem Begin of Israel, and President Anwar Sadat of Egypt end eleven days of discussions at Camp David, Maryland, by signing an accord designed to conclude a peace treaty between Egypt and Israel.

1979: **January 1** The United States officially recognizes the People's Republic of China and terminates its mutual defense treaty with Taiwan.

1979: **August 15** United Nations ambassador Andrew Young resigns following an uproar caused by his meeting with a representative of the Palestine Liberation Organization, a meeting that violated U.S. Middle East policy.

1979: **November 4** In Tehran, Iran, several hundred Iranian militants storm the U.S. embassy and seize the diplomatic personnel. The militants announce they will release the hostages when the United States turns over the former shah of Iran, who is recovering from medical treatment in a New York hospital.

Overview

During the Vietnam War the power of the American government to exert influence overseas was tested in the 1970s as it had not been since World War II (1939–45). And that influence was clearly limited. After the longest war in American history, the United States was unable to win in Vietnam. In 1973, the country settled for a peace treaty that was little more than a piece of paper indicating a failed foreign policy in Asia.

The end of the Vietnam War also closed the deep chasm between Americans who supported the war and those who opposed it. Perhaps at no time since the Civil War (1861–65) had the country been so divided over an issue. Antiwar protestors demonstrated on city streets and on college campuses, leaving some Americans dead at the hands of their fellow countrymen.

During the decade, the United States also suffered continuing trade imbalances and saw a sharp decline in its domination of world markets. There was little the nation could do to alter its trade deficits or its dependence on foreign oil. Its military power was shown to be less dominant, and its economic pressure was shown to be less effective.

In the 1970s, one encouraging development in American foreign policy was the thaw of the cold war (period of extreme political tension between the United States and the Soviet Union following World War II). President Richard M. Nixon recognized that the enormous military spending of the United States and the Soviet Union was bankrupting both countries. Sensing the growing hostilities between the Soviet Union and China, Nixon decided to play the interest of one superpower against the other. He hoped this would lessen the possibility of confronting the Soviets on the battlefield.

By 1972, Nixon had negotiated an arms-control agreement with the Soviet Union and had begun diplomatic talks with China. Presidents Gerald R. Ford and Jimmy Carter tried to continue these initiatives, and for a while they worked. Ultimately, however, the cordial relations among the superpowers cooled yet again as they accused one another of trying to extend their influence around the world. By 1978, Carter was calling for massive increases in military spending, and the world settled in for another decade of the cold war.

The decade found Americans as troubled by domestic issues as by foreign affairs. Their faith in the federal government, already badly shaken by the Vietnam War, was almost completely lost over the events surrounding the 1972 burglary of the Democratic National Committee's headquarters in the Watergate office complex. The arrest of five men in the break-in led to the uncovering of a trail that went all the way to the White House, and right to the Oval Office. Try as he might, Nixon could not hide his involvement in the illegal activities surrounding the case. Faced with mounting evidence and certain impeachment, Nixon created history one last time by resigning from the presidency.

The U.S. Supreme Court played a decisive role in the downfall of the Nixon presidency, and it also was instrumental in resolving conflicts confronting American society in the 1970s. Rapidly growing prison populations and frequent riots raised questions about prison conditions and stricter sentencing to try to reduce rising crime rates. Debates about school busing and school desegregation were conducted in courtrooms and in the streets. And environmental groups and businesses fought legal battles to protect the environment.

The most far-reaching Supreme Court ruling in the decade came in the 1973 *Roe* v. *Wade* case. Many Americans believed that control over childbearing was an important element of women's privacy and equality. Some argued for a constitutional right to preserve a woman's right to choose to have an abortion. The Court's decision, which established a woman's legal right to choose an abortion during the first trimester of pregnancy, created an ongoing debate that changed the course of national politics.

The decade of the 1970s ended as it had begun for America, with involvement in a crisis abroad. The 1979 seizure of the U.S. embassy and its diplomats by Iranian militants was a striking symbol of how much American power overseas had eroded. The volatile political situation in the Middle East made an American military response unlikely. Yet one occurred, and it ended in disaster. The 1970s came to a close with Americans held hostage in Iran and the country feeling it had become a second-rate power.

Carl Bernstein (1944–) and Bob Woodward (1943–) Carl Bernstein and Bob Woodward, reporters for the *Washington Post,* worked more than twelve hours a day for several months to reveal the true story behind the break-in at Democratic Party headquarters in the Watergate complex in June 1972. They were eventually able to link the burglary to high-ranking officials in the Nixon administration, receiving a Pulitzer Prize in journalism in 1973. The following year, they published *All the President's Men,* which detailed events of the political scandal that led to President Nixon's resignation. *Photo reproduced by permission of Archive Photos, Inc.*

William Calley (1943–) William Calley, a lieutenant in the U.S. Army, had led his platoon and two others into the South Vietnamese village of My (pronounced MEE) Lai on March 16, 1968. Finding only women, children, and old men, Calley and his men nonetheless proceeded to shoot to death over one hundred defenseless villagers. They assaulted and raped many young women and girls. When details of the massacre were made public, Calley was charged with murder. Court-martialed in November 1970, he was found guilty and sentenced to life imprisonment. A federal court overturned Calley's conviction in 1974. *Photo reproduced by permission of the Corbis Corporation.*

Shirley Chisholm (1924–) Shirley Chisholm became the first African American woman to serve in the U.S. Congress when she was elected to the House of Representatives in 1968. Articulate and energetic, she established herself as a vocal defender of women and the poor and an outspoken critic of the Vietnam War and racial discrimination. She gained national recognition for her efforts at reform. In 1972, she launched an inspiring campaign for the Democratic nomination for president. Although she failed to win, she achieved her goal of opening the presidential campaign trail to women and minorities. *Photo reproduced by the Corbis Corporation.*

Leon Jaworski (1905–1982) Leon Jaworski was appointed by the Nixon administration in November 1973 to be special prosecutor in the Watergate case, taking the place of the fired Archibald Cox. Many suspected Jaworski was a supporter of the president and would not pursue the case honestly. Yet he kept Cox's staff, continued his investigation of corruption in the Nixon administration, and subpoenaed the White House for Watergate tapes and documents. Jaworski's unbiased and high-minded approach in pursuing the truth exposed evidence that eventually led to the end of the Nixon presidency. *Photo courtesy of the Library of Congress.*

Henry Kissinger (1923–) Henry Kissinger is widely acknowledged as the most influential foreign-policy figure in the 1970s. He served both as national security advisor (1969–75) and as secretary of state (1973–76). His unusual yet successful diplomatic efforts included surprising initiatives and secret negotiations. Kissinger helped bring about a nuclear arms reductions treaty, improved relations with the Soviet Union and China, and peace in Vietnam (for which he won the Nobel Peace Prize in 1973). He was the only high official in the Nixon administration who was not involved in the Watergate scandal. ***Photo courtesy of the Library of Congress.***

George McGovern (1922–) George McGovern ran as the Democratic Party's candidate for president in 1972. He tailored his campaign to young Americans, supporting integration, busing, legalizing marijuana possession, and an end to the Vietnam War. These issues did not matter to the larger American population, and McGovern lost the election by one of the largest margins in U.S. history. However, his impact on American politics was substantial and lasting. McGovern's emphasis on personal character and morality have become central to presidential politics. ***Photo reproduced by permission of the Corbis Corporation.***

Sarah Weddington (1946–) Lawyer Sarah Weddington, along with her associate Linda Coffee, became increasingly involved in feminist projects in the late 1960s. Convinced that reproductive choice was essential to a woman's rights, the pair decided to represent a woman who sought to have an abortion in Texas, where the procedure was illegal. To protect her privacy, the client was assigned the pseudonym Roe instead of her real last name. Weddington argued the case, *Roe* v. *Wade,* all the way the U.S. Supreme Court. In her first court case, Weddington convinced the justices of a woman's right to have an abortion. ***Photo reproduced by permission of AP/Wide World Photos.***

Andrew Young Jr. (1932–) Andrew Young Jr. became the first African American elected to the U.S. House of Representatives from Atlanta, Georgia, in 1972. Reelected twice, he distinguished himself as a champion of poor people, supporting causes such as the minimum wage, day care, and national health care. In 1977, President Jimmy Carter named Young as U.S. ambassador to the United Nations. Brash and outspoken, he received much criticism for his remarks about racism and human rights violations in many countries around the world. For violating official U.S. foreign policy by meeting with a representative from the Palestine Liberation Organization, Young was forced to resign in 1979.

Topics in the News

THE END OF THE VIETNAM WAR

The Vietnam War (1954–75) was the single greatest political controversy of the early 1970s. The war, supported by very few U.S. international allies, eroded confidence in American power at home and abroad. The enormous financial and human cost of the war jeopardized the readiness of American military forces. The huge and escalating expense of the war fueled inflation (the continuing rise in the general price of goods and services because of an overabundance of available money) and threatened to send the nation into a recession (a period of extended economic decline). In the country, opposition to the war increased steadily each month, dividing the American public and straining the relationship between President Richard M. Nixon (1913–1994) and the U.S. Congress.

President Nixon had been elected in 1968 in part because he hinted that he had a plan to end the war and withdraw American troops from Vietnam "with honor." In fact, Nixon had no such plan. Nixon considered immediate withdrawal from Vietnam impossible. Such a drastic move might trigger a political backlash from American supporters of the war, impairing Nixon's ability to draft domestic legislation and to negotiate with foreign powers, especially the Soviet Union. He also feared that the credibility of the United States as a world power would be undermined. in the absence of a face-saving peace treaty, troop withdrawal would appear to be surrender. Like President Lyndon B. Johnson (1908–1973), Nixon did not want to appear to lose the war in Vietnam. He therefore ruled out immediate withdrawal.

Nixon considered the use of nuclear weapons in Vietnam impossible. He knew their use would only further divide Americans over the war and lead to disastrous political consequences overseas. Nixon also knew that a conventional military victory in Vietnam was unlikely. Immediately following his inauguration in 1969, he had commissioned an independent study to determine how long it might take America to defeat the North Vietnamese using conventional weapons. When completed, the study indicated that the war could last another eight to thirteen years. Knowing the American public would not stand for another decade of war, Nixon realized victory in Vietnam was nearly impossible.

OPPOSITE PAGE A soldier with raised hands guides a medical helicopter through the jungle in order to evacuate wounded soldiers during the Vietnam War. **Reproduced by permission of AP/Wide World Photos.**

Unable to withdraw American troops from Vietnam and equally unable to win the war, Nixon turned to an idea that had been proposed under Johnson. He decided to replace U.S. forces with South Vietnamese troops, gradually withdrawing the United States from Vietnam while continuing to support the non-Communist South Vietnamese government of

Nguyen Van Thieu. Nixon called this program "Vietnamization." He hoped it would accomplish two objectives: reduce the level of domestic opposition to the war in Vietnam by returning American soldiers and maintain foreign credibility by upholding U.S. support for an ally.

Unfortunately, the program faltered badly. The key to the failure of Vietnamization was the weakness of the American-backed Thieu regime. Corrupt and unpopular, Thieu's government was never able to rally the

South Vietnamese against the Communist North. Furthermore, the South Vietnamese army, the Army of the Republic of Vietnam (ARVN), fought poorly, if it fought at all, despite receiving nearly $900 million in aid and a generous supply of military hardware from America each year.

Officials from the United States and North Vietnam had begun peace negotiations in Paris in May 1968. The two sides repeatedly deadlocked over issues as the negotiations went on and on. To force the North Vietnamese to accept a peace proposal, in February 1969, Nixon authorized Operation Menu, the bombing of North Vietnamese bases within Cambodia (a neutral country immediately west of South Vietnam). Nixon believed that bombing Cambodia would effectively limit the ability of the North Vietnamese to launch offensive operations against American soldiers as they withdrew from the country. Over the next four years, U.S. forces dropped more than five hundred thousand tons of bombs on Cambodia. Despite this, the North Vietnamese intensified their ground assaults against South Vietnam. Operation Menu, like Vietnamization, was a failure.

By 1972, only 133,000 U.S. soldiers remained in South Vietnam. The ground war was now almost exclusively the responsibility of South Vietnam. But peace negotiations were stalled, and North Vietnam was massing its soldiers to invade the South. With few American combat troops left in the area, Nixon and his administration believed North Vietnam might have a chance to win the war. To counter the North Vietnamese offensive, Nixon used the only military tool left to him: an intensive bombing campaign against the North.

The renewed bombing did not force the North Vietnamese back to the negotiating table. Instead, it was the warming relations between the United States and the Communist superpowers China and the Soviet Union that made North Vietnam reconsider its position. Concerned that they might be losing their allies to the United States, North Vietnamese officials became more willing to negotiate. In October 1972, the United States and North Vietnam agreed to a tentative peace proposal that would have left Thieu's government in place in South Vietnam, but would also have allowed Communists to participate in it. Believing the proposal amounted to a surrender, Thieu rejected it, and negotiations broke down again on December 17.

For the next eleven days, the United States embarked on one of the most intensive bombing campaigns in military history. Forty thousand tons of explosives were dropped in the vicinity of Hanoi, the capital of North Vietnam. Over sixteen hundred North Vietnamese were killed. Europeans and many Americans were outraged by the campaign, soon dubbed the "Christmas bombings." When the U.S. Congress reassembled after the holidays, Democrats in both houses voted to end funding for the war effort. Thieu then gave in, and on January 27, 1973, the United States,

Kent State Killings

President Richard M. Nixon believed his slow withdrawal of American troops from Vietnam would limit any criticism his administration might receive over the decision to invade the neutral country of Cambodia. He was wrong. College students had demonstrated against the Vietnam War for years, but when Nixon announced the Cambodia invasion on April 30, 1970, protests exploded on American campuses from Yale to Stanford. More than four hundred universities and colleges shut down as a result of the protests. Many schools canceled their commencement exercises. Even the American press was highly critical of the invasion.

The day after Nixon's announcement, students at Kent State University in Kent, Ohio, began a weekend of antiwar protests that spilled into the city's downtown area. After rocks were thrown and windows were broken, the governor of Ohio sent in the National Guard to restore order. On Monday, May 4, between two thousand and three thousand students gathered on campus to continue the protest. Guardsmen tried in vain to disperse the students, who threw rocks and yelled obscenities. The guardsmen turned, marched up a hill, then suddenly wheeled around and began firing into the crowd. In the barrage, almost seventy bullets were fired. Thirteen students were hit; four of them were killed. Some of those students who had been shot, including two who had been killed, had not been part of the protest crowd, but were merely walking across campus.

No one is sure why the National Guard fired into the crowd that day. No guardsman was ever tried in court or even reprimanded for any wrongdoing. Federal investigations into the matter went unresolved. Nine years after the incident, the state of Ohio issued a statement of regret, but it never apologized for the shootings.

North Vietnam, and South Vietnam signed a peace treaty. For the United States, the war was officially over.

In March 1973, the last American combat soldiers left South Vietnam. Some American military advisers and Marines remained behind to protect U.S. installations. Of the more than 3 million Americans who served in the war, almost 58,000 died and 150,000 were seriously wounded. More than 1,000 were listed as missing in action.

The peace accord signed in Paris did not bring immediate peace to Vietnam. Tensions between the North and the South remained, and military actions continued. On April 29, 1975, the U.S. embassy in Saigon, the capital of South Vietnam, was evacuated. Four U.S. Marines died during the evacuation; they were the last U.S. soldiers killed in the conflict. The next day, the South Vietnamese government surrendered, and the country was united under a Communist government. The Vietnam War had finally come to an end.

DÉTENTE, SALT, AND THE OPENING OF CHINA

When Richard M. Nixon (1913–1994) became president, he was convinced he had an historic opportunity to restructure the international political order. By 1968, the Soviet Union had amassed a nuclear weapon arsenal equal to that of the United States; the days of American military superiority were over. At the same time, diplomatic relations between the Soviet Union and China had deteriorated; the two nations constantly fought along their shared border. Since both the Soviets and the Chinese sought American support, Nixon and U.S. Secretary of State Henry Kissinger believed that the United States could broker conflicts between the Communist giants. They hoped this "triangular diplomacy" among the three nations would balance international power and secure world peace.

Before triangular diplomacy could work, military competition and political tension between the United States and the Soviet Union had to be reduced. Nixon and Kissinger developed a policy of détente (pronounced day-TONT; a lessening of hostility or tension between nations) toward the Soviet Union. The Strategic Arms Limitation Treaty (SALT) negotiations were the key to the policy of détente. The SALT talks, designed to limit the nuclear-arms race, formally began between the two countries in November 1969 and continued throughout most of the 1970s. The SALT discussions acknowledged two simple facts: Both sides possessed enough nuclear weapons to destroy each other many times over, and the costs of continued nuclear production strained on both economies.

After numerous rounds of talks debating the types of weapons to be reduced, as well as the means of verifying arms reductions, the United States and the Soviet Union concluded two treaties: The Antiballistic Missile (ABM) Treaty limited the defensive nuclear weapons available to each nation and the SALT I accord limited the number of offensive missiles. The United States also negotiated trade and financial agreements with the Soviets. Together with the SALT accords, these agreements advanced détente and enhanced Nixon's image as a peacemaker. Nixon used that

Presidential Election Results: 1970s

Presidential Election Results: 1972

Presidential/ Vice Presidential Candidate	Political Party	Popular Vote	Electoral Vote
Richard Nixon/ Spiro Agnew	Republican	47,169,911 (60.69%)	520 (96.6%)
George McGovern/ R. Sargent Shriver	Democrat	29,170,383 (37.53%)	17 (3.2%)
John Hospers/ Theodora Nathan	Libertarian	3,673 (0.00%)	1 (0.2%)
John Schmitz/ Thomas Anderson	Independent	1,099,482 (1.41%)	0 (0.0%)
Other		275,105 (0.35%)	0 (0.0%)

Presidential Election Results: 1976

Presidential/ Vice Presidential Candidate	Political Party	Popular Vote	Electoral Vote
Jimmy Carter/ Walter Mondale	Democrat	40,830,763 (50.06%)	297 (55.2%)
Gerald Ford/ Robert Dole	Republican	39,147,793 (48.00%)	240 (44.6%)
Ronald Reagan/ Robert Dole	Republican		1 (0.2%)
Eugene McCarthy/ Various	Independent	756,691 (0.93%)	0 (0.0%)
Other		820,642 (1.01%)	0 (0.0%)

image to his political advantage. He signed SALT in a highly publicized visit to Moscow in May 1972, the presidential election year.

For more than two decades, Nixon had crafted his political reputation as a formidable opponent of Communist China. Now, in order to make triangular diplomacy work, Nixon had to become the president who restored diplomatic relations with that country (those relations had been

Richard M. Nixon

Richard M. Nixon suffered the greatest humiliation in U.S. political history; he was the first president to resign the office. The defeat was doubly crushing for Nixon because he destroyed himself. His own paranoid need to protect himself with secret tapes gave his enemies the tools to undermine him. Had Nixon been slightly less ruthless with his opponents, they might have been less ruthless with him. Despite a career in politics championing the common man, Nixon's own distrust of the American people prevented him from being frank with them. This need for secrecy, more than any other characteristic, brought about his political downfall.

Nixon was born on January 9, 1913, in Yorba Linda, California, to Quaker parents. Armed from a young age with a strong drive to succeed, Nixon earned good grades at school while working long hours in his family's grocery and gas station. His drive and ambition distinguished him at Duke University Law School, but he failed to obtain a job with any of the prestigious East Coast law firms he approached after graduation. He returned to California, married Pat Ryan, a schoolteacher, then enlisted in the U.S. Navy during World War II (1939–45).

After the war, in 1946, Nixon was elected to his first political office as a Republican in the U.S. House of Representatives. During his time in the House, Nixon portrayed himself as the champion of the common man, hardworking and patriotic. Although he

cut off in 1949 when the Communists came to power in China). Nixon's initial overtures to Chinese officials were secret, but the Chinese responded positively, and on June 10, 1971 Nixon announced he would drop the twenty-one-year-old embargo on American trade with China. Kissinger, in the meantime, was secretly negotiating the terms of a state visit to Beijing (formerly Peking), the Chinese capital.

When Nixon informed the American public that he would journey to China, the news came as a surprise, but the majority of the public responded favorably. Public opinion was overwhelmingly positive toward Nixon's

knew little about communism, Nixon took advantage of the anticommunist wave sweeping America at the time. He accused many of his political opponents of being communists. In 1950, after his election to the U.S. Senate, he became a national political star for his incessant hounding of Alger Hiss, a former State Department official, accusing Hiss of being a communist and a Soviet spy.

In 1952, Nixon was tapped to be Dwight D. Eisenhower's running mate for the presidency. With the national visibility he gained as vice president, Nixon was easily the Republican front-runner in the 1960 presidential campaign. Compared to his Democratic opponent John F. Kennedy, however, Nixon was a less effective speaker and a less appealing figure. In response, American voters gave Kennedy an extremely narrow margin of victory, and Nixon returned to California. When he lost the run for the California governorship just two years later, it seemed Nixon's political career was over.

Yet, in 1968, Nixon staged a remarkable comeback, winning the presidential election over Democrat Hubert Humphrey on a strong law-and-order campaign platform. Once in office, Nixon faced many difficult issues: the Vietnam War, a declining economy, and tense relations with the Soviet Union and China. Instead of highlighting his solutions to these problems, Nixon focused on silencing dissent, crushing his political opponents, and settling old scores. When he was forced to resign the presidency on August 9, 1974, in the wake of the Watergate scandal, he was, without a doubt, one of the most reviled political figures in the United States.

Nixon died of a stroke in New York City on April 22, 1994. ***Photo courtesy of the Library of Congress.***

journey to China in February 1972. Images of the trip, broadcast live via the latest satellite technology, awed the American people. Beyond the images, however, the trip accomplished little. Formal recognition by the United States of the People's Republic of China (the formal name of Communist China) did not occur until 1979. The images of Nixon in China, however, did advance the cause of triangular diplomacy and increased Soviet willingness to negotiate with the Americans. In the end, the most important audience for the trip was the millions of American voters waiting to cast their ballots in the fall election; Nixon was reelected by a landslide.

George C. Wallace

George C. Wallace was a towering and highly controversial figure in politics in the South for decades. In the 1970s, he made a bid for the presidency, hoping to court those Americans who were opposed to increased governmental power and sick of the cultural revolutions of the 1960s. But a nearly fatal assassination attempt during his campaign ended his dreams of wielding power in the White House.

Born in Clio, Alabama, on August 25, 1919, Wallace received a law degree from the University of Alabama, then joined the U.S. military. After World War II (1939–45) he began a political career, serving as assistant attorney general of Alabama (1946–47), a member of the state assembly of Alabama (1947–53), and governor of Alabama (1963–67, 1971–79, 1983–87).

In 1963, Wallace achieved national prominence when he stood in the entrance to the University of Alabama and defied President John F. Kennedy's order to integrate the school. He quickly became known as an opponent of federal power. He also became known as a champion of segregation, a man who opposed the advancement of rights for African Americans.

WATERGATE AND THE RESIGNATION OF NIXON

At 2:00 A.M. on Saturday, June 17, 1972, four Cubans and a member of the Committee to Reelect the President, James W. McCord, were arrested for burglarizing the offices of the Democratic National Committee, located in the Watergate office complex in Washington, D.C. The burglary would lead to the first resignation of a president in American history and expose to the public a dark underside of politics they scarcely knew existed. Public cynicism about politics after Watergate would affect not only Richard M. Nixon (1913–1994) but also his successors, Gerald R. Ford (1913–) and Jimmy Carter (1924–).

In early 1972, President Nixon was unsure of his prospects for reelection that fall. Members of his Committee to Reelect the President (CREEP) therefore hatched plots to wiretap the offices of Democratic presidential candidate George McGovern and Democratic National Committee chairman Lawrence O'Brien. Both attempts failed. The arrest for the second CREEP break-in, at O'Brien's office in the Watergate, resulted from a bungled attempt to replace a defective hidden listening device. Six days

In 1968, Wallace ran as an independent candidate for president on his own American Independent Party ticket. Speaking out against African Americans, students, and protestors of the Vietnam War, he was able to win five southern states and forty-six electoral votes during his campaign. Four years later, he ran again. He made a strong start, mobilizing fundamentalist Christians and earning support in the North and South for his opposition to school busing. On May 15, 1972, during a campaign stop in Laurel, Maryland, his candidacy ended abruptly when he was shot by Arthur Bremer. Wallace was left paralyzed in both legs, and was lucky to be alive.

Confined to a wheelchair, Wallace made another bid for the presidency in 1976, but his fragile health and his ultra-conservative views brought a quick end to his campaign. In 1982, he ran for governor of Alabama for a fourth, and final, time. Admitting that his past racial views had been wrong, Wallace won with the support of many of the state's African American voters. He retired in 1987.

Wallace died in Montgomery, Alabama, on September 13, 1998.

later, Nixon directed his staff to block an FBI investigation of the case and cover up the connections between the burglars and CREEP. This order was the first of many attempts to obstruct justice by the most powerful law-enforcement official in the United States.

Nixon ordered a cover-up because he feared that an investigation into the Watergate break-in would expose the numerous illegal activities of his administration. During the campaign, Democrats charged that Watergate represented wider lawbreaking. Their allegations were ignored, and the break-in had no adverse effect on Nixon's election victory. The story would have died were it not for the criminal trial of the Watergate burglars and for two reporters from the *Washington Post,* Bob Woodward and Carl Bernstein, who dug deeper into the case. Together with the federal judge, John J. Sirica, who presided over the criminal trial, they kept the pressure on the White House for an explanation of the break-in and of McCord's connections to CREEP.

Nixon's administration tried to suggest to the public that McCord or his superiors in CREEP ordered the break-in without the president's knowledge. CREEP immediately renounced McCord (even as it secretly paid his legal fees). Yet Woodward and Bernstein kept discovering evidence that indicated top-level administration officials knew about and authorized the Watergate break-in. One by one, connections between the burglars and their superiors in CREEP were disclosed. As the incriminating evidence mounted, members of Nixon's staff then moved to protect themselves from criminal prosecution. Resignations became commonplace. CREEP chairman John Mitchell and CREEP treasurer Hugh Sloan quit their positions in the fall of 1972. White House chief of staff H. R. Haldeman, domestic-policy assistant John Ehrlichman, presidential counsel John Dean, and Attorney General Richard Kleindienst resigned on April 30, 1973.

McCord informed Judge Sirica that members of the Nixon administration had committed perjury (lied under oath) during his criminal trial. No one in the conspiracy was willing to take the blame for the crime, and eventually Woodward and Bernstein raised the following questions: What did the president know, and when did he know it? The Democrats and the U.S. Congress also wanted to know the answer to these questions. On February 7, 1973, the U.S. Senate voted seventy to zero to establish a seven-man investigative committee, headed by Senator Sam Ervin of North Carolina, to probe the Watergate case. Immediately following his second inauguration, after one of the greatest electoral victories in American history, Nixon was fighting for his political life.

In May 1973, the U.S. Department of Justice authorized a special prosecutor, Archibald Cox, to study Watergate without interference from the White House. Startling revelations about the Nixon administration began to mount. The Ervin committee's televised hearings climaxed in the stunning testimony of White House counsel Dean, which connected the president to the Watergate cover-up. Even more damaging was the public testimony of White House aide Alexander Butterfield on July 16. He revealed the existence of a secret recording system installed in the White House. Unbelievably, presidential decisions regarding Watergate had been recorded on tape.

Ervin, Cox, and Sirica immediately pressed the White House to release the Watergate tapes to them. Nixon rejected their requests, claiming the tapes were private property. He also asserted that the tapes contained material that might compromise national security. Furthermore, he argued that he had a right to withhold them under the supposed constitutional claim of executive privilege (an idea that the president could decide for himself how much he might cooperate with other branches of the government). The press charged the president with stonewalling (stalling and refusing to answer questions), preventing access to the truth. Nixon's popularity with the American public plummeted to below 40 percent.

Richard Nixon leaving the White House after resigning the presidency due to the Watergate scandal. **Reproduced by permission of AP/Wide World Photos.**

On October 12, the U.S. District Court of Appeals ordered Nixon to turn over the Watergate tapes to Cox and Sirica. Instead, Nixon proposed releasing prepared transcripts of the tapes. The decision infuriated Cox, who attacked the administration for not complying. Nixon responded by ordering Cox to be fired, but Attorney General Elliot Richardson refused. Nixon then fired Richardson and ordered Deputy Attorney General William Ruckelshaus to fire Cox. Ruckelshaus also refused, and Nixon fired Ruckelshaus. Nixon finally persuaded Solicitor General Robert Bork to dismiss Cox. The public was outraged, and the press termed the firings the "Saturday Night Massacre."

In an effort to turn the tide of public opinion, Nixon released a 1,308-page edited transcript of the Watergate tapes on April 29, 1974. He maintained that the transcripts proved that he did not know about the Watergate cover-up until March 21, 1973. Nixon hoped the publication of the transcripts would restore public confidence in his honesty; instead, the highly edited transcripts embarrassed the president and made him the object of ridicule.

The new special prosecutor, Leon Jaworski, pursued the Watergate investigation as intensely as Cox had. But he doubted that a sitting president could be subject to criminal indictment (formal accusation) by a grand jury. Under the U.S. Constitution, only the U.S. Congress could indict a president for criminal wrongdoing, a process known as impeachment. During the impeachment process, the U.S. House of Representatives determines whether an indictment is justified, and then the chief justice of the U.S. Supreme Court presides over a trial, with the U.S. Senate acting as jury. If the president is found guilty of high crimes or misdemeanors, he can be removed from office.

On July 24, 1974, in *United States* v. *Richard M. Nixon,* the U.S. Supreme Court unanimously upheld the constitutionality of executive privilege, but denied that it applied to the Watergate tapes. They ordered Nixon to turn over all the tapes to special prosecutor Jaworski. Then on July 30, the House Judiciary Committee recommended to the full House that it vote to impeach the president for three offenses: obstruction of justice, abuse of power, and contempt of Congress (behavior that threatens Congress's legislative power). With the Supreme Court ruling against him and the House about to vote on his impeachment, Nixon was trapped and he knew it.

On August 5, the transcripts became available to the public, and they showed that the president had ordered a cover-up. Nixon's defenders were stunned, and leading Republicans went to the White House to report that he had lost all remaining congressional support. On August 8, in a televised address, Nixon resigned the presidency, effective at noon the following day. Vice President Gerald R. Ford then became the thirty-eighth president of the United States (Ford had assumed the office when former Vice President Spiro Agnew resigned in October 1973 after he had pleaded guilty to income-tax evasion). One month later, on September 8, to spare Nixon from criminal prosecution for obstruction of justice, Ford granted Nixon a "full, free, and absolute pardon."

ROE V. *WADE:* THE ABORTION CONTROVERSY

In late 1969, Norma McCorvey, twenty-one and single, found herself facing an unwanted pregnancy. She already had a five-year-old daughter whom she could not support financially. McCorvey's mother had taken custody of the child. Working as a waitress in a bar, she had little money and nowhere to go. Believing she was not in any condition to care for another child, McCorvey wanted to end her pregnancy through an abortion. However, in Texas, where she lived, an abortion was allowed only for a woman whose life was endangered by her pregnancy; McCorvey's was not.

Then McCorvey met Linda Coffee, a young attorney concerned about feminist issues. Among other things, Coffee believed that equality would not be possible for women until they had control over their reproductive status. Along with Sarah Weddington, a law-school classmate, Coffee wanted to challenge Texas's abortion statutes in court as unconstitutional. Once the pair met McCorvey, they knew they had found a case. Weddington and Coffee warned her that the decision would not come fast enough to allow her actually to have an abortion; McCorvey would almost certainly have to agree to give birth. She did. Concerned about publicity, McCorvey agreed to be a plaintiff (person who brings a lawsuit against another in a civil court) only if the lawsuit did not use her name. Norma McCorvey thus became Jane Roe, and her lawsuit became *Roe* v. *Wade* (Henry Wade was the Texas district attorney arguing in favor of the state's abortion laws).

At this time in the United States, abortion laws varied from state to state. Some states (such as Texas) prohibited all abortions except those to save a woman's life. Others permitted abortions if a doctor found that the pregnancy threatened a woman's life, if the fetus were likely to be born deformed, or if the pregnancy were the result of rape or incest.

The U.S. Supreme Court had previously decided cases that indicated it might be willing to rule against antiabortion statutes such as those in Texas. In 1968, the Court held in *Griswold* v. *Connecticut* that a state could not prohibit the sale of contraceptives to married people. This decision held that the U.S. Constitution implicitly recognized a right to privacy. In 1971, in *Eisenstadt* v. *Baird,* the Court went even further, extending that right to unmarried people. The stage seemed to be set for a more sweeping ruling regarding reproduction and the right to privacy.

On January 22, 1973, the Supreme Court handed down a decision in *Roe* v. *Wade*. In its historic ruling, the Court found that the Fourteenth Amendment of the U.S. Constitution provided a fundamental right to privacy under which women could obtain abortions. The Court decreed that the decision to have an abortion during the first three months of pregnancy, known as the first trimester, was a choice to be made privately between a woman and her doctor.

Although the Court's decision legalized abortion throughout the country, it did not grant women unrestricted access to abortions. Since the fetus is viable, or able to survive outside the womb, during the last ten weeks, the Court allowed any state to prohibit abortion during this period, except where it might be necessary to preserve the life or health of the woman. States may apply other restrictions between the first trimester and the last ten weeks of pregnancy, such as licensing and regulating abortion providers.

Many supporters of abortion restrictions were shocked by the decision establishing a right to abortion. The antiabortion movement referred

Environmental Law

The debate over environmental protection in America intensified during the 1970s, and much of that debate took place in the courts. The U.S. Congress passed several statutes that gave the judicial branch a central role in environmental enforcement. The National Environmental Policy Act (NEPA) of 1970 required the federal government to write an environmental impact statement for all "federal projects with a significant environmental impact." Supporters or opponents of a project could go to court to challenge the claims of the impact statement regarding that particular project. The Clean Air Act amendments of 1970 required the Environmental Protection Agency to set health-based standards for local air quality. The Water Pollution Control Act amendments of 1972 imposed similar requirements for water pollution. These standards could be challenged, either by environmental groups or by companies required to reduce their pollution. As a result, the courts became a principal battleground in the struggle over environmental regulation. During the 1970s, there were 855 federal lawsuits involving NEPA—233 involving clean air and 508 involving clean water.

to itself as pro-life, attempting to implicate its opponents as advocates of death. Those who supported a woman's right to abortion insisted that they were not necessarily in favor of abortion but of the right of a woman to choose for herself whether she should bear a child. These advocates called themselves pro-choice. The struggle between the groups was intense.

In spite of general support in America for the right to an abortion, the antiabortion movement was able to organize in response to the Court's ruling. Challenging the exact terms of the ruling, the antiabortion movement convinced the legislatures in several states to enact laws requiring consent from the parents of minors, the spouse, or the prospective father before an abortion could be performed. However, in 1976, in *Planned Parenthood* v. *Danforth,* the Supreme Court struck down these consent provisions as too restrictive of a woman's right to an abortion.

While the *Roe* v. *Wade* decision prevented states from outlawing abortions, it did not require that states pay for them. In 1976, the antiabortion movement persuaded the U.S. Congress to pass the so-called Hyde amendment to the Medicaid funding bill, which forbade the use of federal funds to pay for an abortion except when a woman's life was in danger. Antiabortionists also pressured individual states to take similar steps to refuse to pay for abortions except for life-saving reasons. In 1980, the Supreme Court upheld the Hyde amendment.

The *Roe* v. *Wade* decision was one of the most important, and controversial, rulings in U.S. Supreme Court history. The political and legal struggles that arose from it continued to be a defining element of American politics in the rest of the twentieth century.

THE IRAN HOSTAGE CRISIS

In 1941, Muhammad Reza Pahlavi (1919–1980) became shah, or monarch, of Iran. Unlike his father, whom he succeeded to the throne, Muhammad Reza Pahlavi was open to Western ideas (he had been educated in Switzerland). He quickly became an ally of the United States and other Western powers who had a great stake in Iran's oil industry. In 1953, with American help, the shah foiled his prime minister's plans to nationalize (put under government control) the property of foreign oil companies in Iran. During the 1950s and 1960s, the shah purchased billions of dollars' worth of American

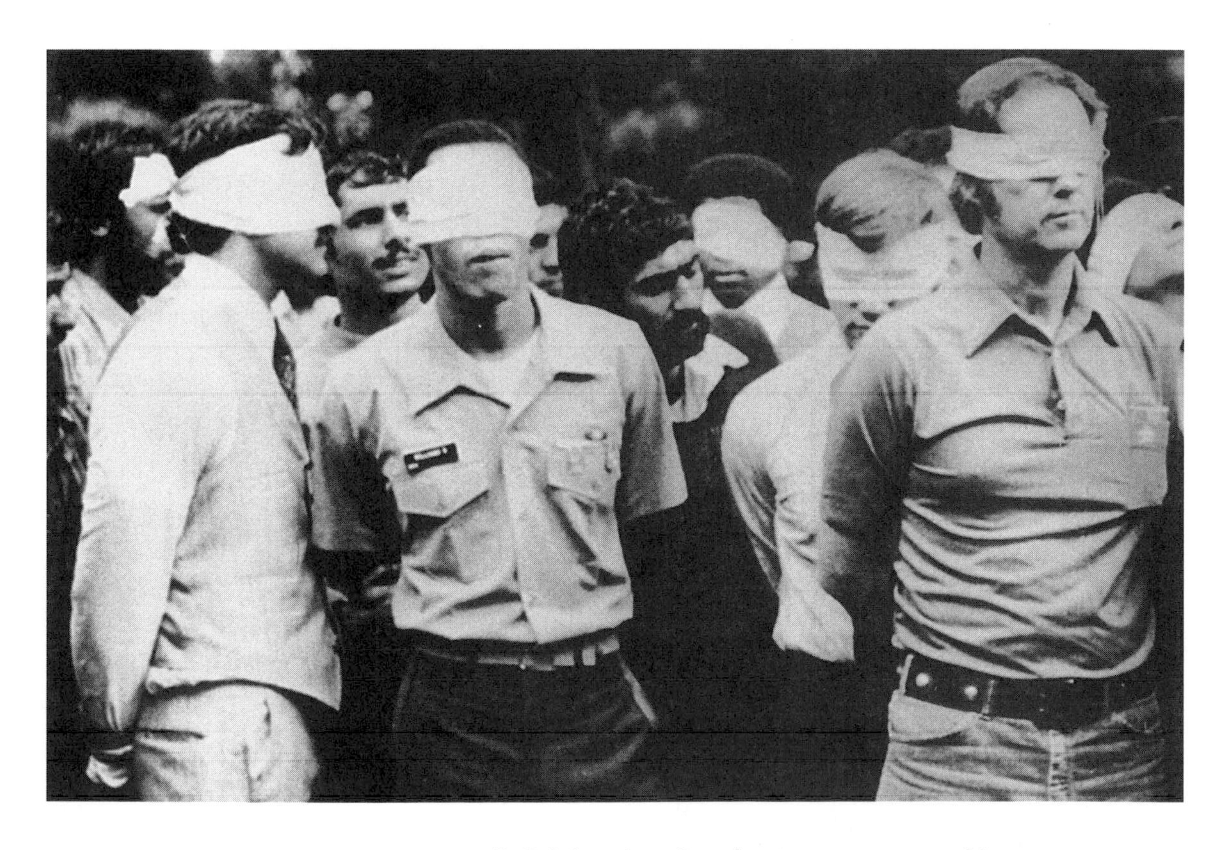

U.S. embassy hostages blindfolded and bound during the Iran hostage crisis, which lasted from 1979 to 1981. **Reproduced by permission of the Corbis Corporation.**

The Attica Riot

During the summer of 1971, tension and unrest were building the Attica State Correctional Facility in Attica, New York. The prison was overcrowded, housing 2,250 men in a facility considered safe for only 1,600 inmates. Racial tensions were also high. The prison had no African American guards and only one Puerto Rican guard, yet the inmates were 54 percent black and 9 percent Puerto Rican. On September 9, minor disciplinary actions against two inmates for fighting erupted quickly into a full-scale riot involving more than one thousand inmates who took control of the prison, setting fire to several buildings. Fifty prison guards were taken as hostages, most of whom were beaten by angry inmates. Several seriously injured hostages were released, and one hostage died as a result of his injuries.

The inmates quickly organized a negotiating team and drew up demands. These included complete amnesty (general pardon) for participants in the riot, federal takeover of the prison, better living conditions in the prison, and removal of the prison's superintendent. State officials refused a complete amnesty from criminal prosecution for the riot and the removal of the prison superintendent. Negotiations stalled at this point. State officials then presented an ultimatum to the inmates: either accept the offer or have the prison retaken by force. The inmates refused to accept.

arms and tried to modernize his country's agricultural, industrial, and economic systems. However, social classes in Iran became further segregated as money from the oil industry was distributed unequally among the people, resulting in a small wealthy class. In addition, the fundamentalist Islamic clergy in Iran began to criticize the shah's pro-Western political policies.

By the 1970s, a political and cultural backlash led by Islamic religious fundamentalists began to grow. In an effort to contain this backlash, the shah resorted to increasingly oppressive measures. Often, he used SAVAK, his harsh secret police force, to put down any rebellion. This tactic only succeeded in alienating his fellow Iranians to the point of revolution. By 1978, riots were breaking out all over the country, and many Iranians called for the return of Shi'ite religious leader Ayatollah Ruhollah Khomeini (1900–1989), who had been exiled (banished) to France in 1964.

On the morning of September 13, New York governor Nelson Rockefeller ordered state police, sheriffs' deputies, and correctional officers to launch an attack on the area of the prison controlled by inmates. They first fired tear gas into the cell blocks. Officers then fired rifles and shotguns into the prison yard from roofs and other high points. The attack lasted ten minutes. Initial reports stated that nine hostages had their throats slashed by inmates. Later investigations made clear that inmates had not killed any hostages during the attack. Instead, ten hostages had been killed by gunshots from the police and prison guards retaking the prison yard. Twenty-nine inmates were killed in the attack.

New York State officials were heavily criticized for the attack and for the prison conditions that had led to the riot in the first place. Attica came to symbolize the dangerous conditions of many prisons in America and the restrictions on prisoners' religious and political freedoms. The Attica riot provoked several efforts to reform prison conditions across the United States. Those reform efforts often failed because of budget limitations and escalating prison populations, which increased prison overcrowding. Prison conditions and overcrowding were considered more of a problem at the end of the 1970s than they were at the time of the Attica riot.

On January 16, 1979, the shah fled Iran. Khomeini returned to the country and assumed control, declaring Iran an Islamic republic. In September, ill with cancer, the shah was admitted to a New York hospital. In response, on November 4, a mob of Islamic militants seized the U.S. embassy in Tehran, the capital of Iran. They ultimately detained fifty-two members of the American consulate as hostages, demanding the return of the shah to face trial in exchange for the release of the hostages. They also demanded the return of billions of dollars the shah alleged took with him when he fled Iran.

President Jimmy Carter (1924–) refused to be blackmailed into returning the shah, who eventually died in Egypt in 1980. Because the hostage-taking violated diplomatic convention and international law, Carter was able to rally world opinion against Iran, imposing an economic embargo and freezing Iranian funds in foreign banks. But he was unable to win release of the hostages through diplomatic means. On April 24, 1980,

Carter authorized a military rescue mission, against the advice of U.S. Secretary of State Cyrus Vance. This mission was a disaster: Three of the eight helicopters sent in crashed during a sandstorm, killing eight U.S. soldiers.

As the crisis dragged on without resolution, many Americans concluded Carter was inept. The hostage-taking fatally undermined his presidency and became a major factor in his loss to Ronald Reagan (1911–) in the 1980 presidential election. The Iran hostage crisis came to an end on the day of President Reagan's inauguration, January 20, 1981, after the United States released almost eight billion dollars in frozen Iranian assets. The hostages had been held captive for 444 days.

For More Information

BOOKS

Bernstein, Carl, and Bob Woodward. *All the President's Men*. New York: Simon and Schuster, 1999.

Carroll, Peter N. *It Seemed Like Nothing Happened: America in the 1970s*. Piscataway, NJ: Rutgers University Press, 1990.

Fremon, David K. *The Watergate Scandal in American History*. Berkeley Heights, NJ: Enslow, 1998.

Gordon, William A. *Four Dead in Ohio: Was There a Conspiracy at Kent State?* Lake Forest, CA: North Ridge Books, 1995.

Larsen, Rebecca. *Richard Nixon: Rise and Fall of a President*. New York: Franklin Watts, 1991.

Marrin, Albert. *America and Vietnam: The Elephant and the Tiger*. New York: Viking, 1992.

Stevens, Leonard A. *The Case of Roe v. Wade*. New York: Philomel Books, 1996.

WEB SITES

The American Experience/Vietnam. http://www.pbs.org/wgbh/amex/vietnam/index.html (accessed on March 14, 2002).

CNN-Roe vs. Wade-1998. http://www.cnn.com/SPECIALS/1998/roe.wade/ (accessed on March 17, 2002).

Dave Leip's Atlas of U.S. Presidential Elections. http://www.uselectionatlas.org/USPRESIDENT/frametextj.html (accessed on March 13, 2002).

Iranian Hostage Crisis. http://www.louisville.edu/library/ekstrom/govpubs/subjects/hist/iranhostage.html (accessed on March 17, 2002).

May4.Net. http://64.224.189.204/home.asp (accessed on March 16, 2002).

SALT I. http://www.state.gov/www/global/arms/treaties/salt1.html (accessed on March 15, 2002).

The Watergate Decade. http://www.journale.com/watergate.html (accessed March 15, 2002).

Watergate—The Scandal That Destroyed President Richard Nixon. http://www.watergate.info/ (accessed on March 15, 2002).

chapter five

Lifestyles and Social Trends

Chronology

1970: For the first time in American history, a majority of Americans live in suburbs.

1970: Police touch off a riot in the barrio of East Los Angeles, resulting in the death of prominent Hispanic journalist Ruben Salazar and inspiring the growing Chicano consciousness movement.

1970: **August 29** A parade of ten thousand women in New York celebrates the fiftieth anniversary of the passage of the Nineteenth Amendment to the U.S. Constitution, which gave women the right to vote; the women demand abortion reform, day care, and equal opportunity.

1971: The Twenty-Sixth Amendment to the U.S. Constitution, lowering the voting age form twenty-one to eighteen, is ratified.

1971: Hot pants, very brief shorts for women, become a fashion sensation.

1971: In *Reed* v. *Reed,* the U.S. Supreme Court bans gender discrimination.

1971: In Chicago, the Reverend Jesse Jackson forms People United to Save Humanity (PUSH).

1972: The U.S. Congress approves the Equal Rights Amendment (ERA) and sends it to the states to be ratified.

1972: Protesting Native Americans march in Washington, D.C.

1972: The U.S. Congress passes the Ethnic Heritage Studies Act "to legitimatize ethnicity and pluralism in America."

1972: Phyllis Schlafly organizes the National Committee to Stop the ERA.

1973: The American Psychiatric Association rules that homosexuality is not a mental disorder.

1973: Three men are sworn in as the first African American mayors in their respective large cities: Maynard Jackson in Atlanta, Thomas Bradley in Los Angeles, and Coleman Young in Detroit.

1974: A fad known as "streaking," where people sprint naked through public places and events, sweeps the country.

1974: Maternity leave for teachers is approved by the U.S. Supreme Court.

1974: **February 4** In Berkeley, California, nineteen-year-old newspaper heiress Patricia Hearst is kidnapped by the Symbionese Liberation Army.

1975: Twenty million mood rings, a type of jewelry that changes color with body temperature, are sold in the United States.

1975: The pet rock, an elaborately packaged stone, becomes a popular holiday gift.

1975: Polyester and mixed-blend fabrics become popular in both men's and women's wear.

1975: **July 2** The United Nations-sponsored International Women's Year Conference meeting ends in Mexico City.

1976: Punk fashions from London arrive in American shops.

1976: The National Aeronautics and Space Administration (NASA) accepts its first female astronaut trainees.

1976: **September 18** The Reverend Sun Myung Moon presides over a God Bless America rally in Washington, D.C. Fifty thousand followers of Moon attend.

1977: Twenty-five million CB (citizens' band) radios are in use by American motorists

1977: Diane Keaton, in her starring role in the film *Annie Hall*, catapults Ralph Lauren's rumpled men's look for women to high fashion.

1977: **April 16** Steve Rubell and Ian Shrager open the doors of Studio 54, the exclusive New York discotheque.

1978: In Washington, D.C., sixty-five thousand women march in support of the Equal Rights Amendment (ERA).

1978: After a popular exhibit of Egyptian relics travels to several major U.S. museums, a "King Tut" craze sweeps the nation.

1978: **October 6** At the University of Chicago, Hannah H. Gray is inaugurated as the first female president of a coed university.

1978: **November 18** Authorities discover the mass suicides and murders of over nine hundred members of Jim Jones's People's Temple cult in Guyana.

1979: Over 14.5 million Americans identify themselves as Hispanic.

1979: Jerry Falwell organizes the conservative Moral Majority political lobbying group.

1979: One hundred thousand people march in Washington, D.C., in support of gay liberation.

1979: **April 3** Jane Byrne is elected Chicago's first female mayor, winning the election by the largest majority since 1901.

Overview

The decade of the 1970s was in many ways a continuation of the late 1960s with respect to social trends. The activists of the 1960s crusaded for social justice in the 1970s, gaining new freedoms for women, Native Americans, Hispanic Americans, homosexuals, the elderly, and other ethnic and minority groups.

Of all the movements, women's liberation remained the most controversial and far-reaching. In the 1970s, women's groups tried to create a more open and nurturing society. To achieve this, they demanded and won access to male-dominated business and universities. Woman also made inroads into politics at the local, state, and national levels. They became doctors, lawyers, teachers, priests, scientists, writers, plumbers, dock workers, pilots, stockbrokers, and sports heroes. By breaking down employment barriers and expanding opportunities, women transformed the character of the American family.

Women's liberation and other social-justice movements became the focus of heated opposition. Conservatives were uncomfortable with the changing American society of the 1970s, especially those changes initiated by the youth counterculture of the 1960s. They believed these changes caused social problems such as a rise in the crime rate, a greater number of poor people, a less motivated work force, and a decline in moral values.

Trying to swing the social pendulum back from the far left, conservatives were joined by former liberal Democrats, a group that became known as neoconservatives. These "new" conservatives, while retaining their liberal views on certain matters, were disturbed by certain social reforms of the 1960s, which they believed went too far. These groups together called for a return to what they called cultural traditionalism.

Joining conservatives and neoconservatives in their fight against social change in America were various religious groups, which began to wield significant political power. With three recessions, double-digit inflation, and double-digit unemployment, the 1970s was a period of economic upheaval. Facing an uncertain future, many Americans were drawn to the stability of traditional values and fundamentalist Christian teachings.

Other Americans turned away from the problems of society, focusing on themselves instead. Seeking to fill their lives with meaning, they experimented with exercise, psychotherapy, health food, and alternative religions. In their search for spiritual fulfillment, many people began to follow the teachings of self-anointed prophets and spiritual gurus. Although some of these spiritual leaders were legitimate, others were unethical con men, using their followers' financial contributions to fund a lavish personal lifestyle. A few were dangerous madmen, leading their unsuspecting believers to their death.

Almost all aspects of American society in the 1970s were marked by a restlessness and a questioning of traditional authority. From public protest movements to personal fashion, people sought a means of self-expression. Breaking traditional fashion rules, women and men experimented with how they looked: They combined separates rather than wearing suits, drew influences from other cultures and time periods, wore pants or dresses, threw away ties and jackets, and walked around in athletic wear. Throughout the decade, people dressed however they wanted, and what they wanted most was comfort and a unique style.

Bella Abzug (1920–1998) In 1970, in her first political campaign, Bella Abzug was elected to the U.S. House of Representatives. One of only twelve women elected to serve in the House at the time, she was the first Jewish women elected to Congress. Flamboyant in appearance and outspoken in temperament, Abzug disregarded her freshman status in the House and assumed a leadership role in the Vietnam War protest and women's rights movements. A year after losing her bid for reelection in 1976, she became cochair of the President's National Advisory Committee on Women, serving until 1979. *Photo reproduced by permission of AP/Wide World Photos.*

Jim Bakker (1940–) and Tammy Faye Bakker (1942–) In 1972, Jim Bakker and Tammy Faye Bakker began broadcasting their Christian television talk show, *The PTL Club.* Two years later, they set up their own broadcasting system, the PTL Network. The Bakkers quickly became celebrities, and contributions to their show soon topped five million dollars. In 1978, the Bakkers began to build Heritage USA, a planned community for Christians. By the end of the decade, however, the Bakkers' lavish lifestyle and questionable fund-raising tactics prompted an investigation by the Federal Communications Commission. The investigation would eventually lead to their downfall. *Photo reproduced by permission of AP/Wide World Photos.*

Cesar Chavez (1927–1993) Cesar Chavez was the most effective labor leader of the 1970s. He rose from poverty as an Hispanic migrant worker in Arizona to international celebrity as the leader of the United Farm Workers (UFW) union. He promoted social change through nonviolent means, and he organized workers and supporters across ethnic, class, and gender lines. These tactics, which went against current approaches, not only improved working conditions for members of the UFW but also inspired respect and admiration throughout the country. *Photo reproduced by permission of AP/Wide World Photos.*

Patricia Hearst (1953–) Patricia Hearst, the daughter of wealthy newspaper publisher William Randolph Hearst, was involved in one of the more bizarre events of the 1970s. In February 1974, the Symbionese Liberation Army (SLA), a leftist terrorist group, kidnapped her and held her for two million dollars' ransom. After her parents failed to negotiate her release, Hearst was allegedly brainwashed by the SLA. In April of that year, she assisted the group in a San Francisco bank robbery. A year later, police captured Hearst, and she was sentenced to seven years in prison for the crime. She was released in 1979. *Photo reproduced by permission of Archive Photos, Inc.*

Jesse Jackson (1941–) In the 1970s, Jesse Jackson was the most visible civil rights leader in the country. His organization, Operation PUSH (People United to Save Humanity), founded in 1971, sought to strengthen the economic position of African Americans. Among other issues, Operation PUSH pressed larger businesses to hire more minorities and work more closely with minority businesses. In 1975, Jackson brought national attention to the subject of minority education, raising money for an elementary school program called PUSH for Excellence, or PUSH-EXCEL. The aim of the program was to revive pride and self-discipline among students in inner-city schools. *Photo courtesy of the Library of Congress.*

Calvin Klein (1942–) In 1972, fashion designer Calvin Klein began creating his flexible collections of interchangeable separates, mainly for women, that were both casual and elegant. That same year, he also launched his line of sportswear separates that could be intermixed to produce a complete day and evening wardrobe. His clothes helped reinvigorate American fashion design at a time when most young Americans cared little about the industry. Beginning in 1973, Klein received three consecutive prestigious Coty awards, becoming the youngest designer to be so honored. In the late 1970s, Klein introduced the first designer jeans, changing the way jeans were perceived thereafter. *Photo reproduced by permission of the Corbis Corporation.*

Ralph Lauren (1939–) Ralph Lauren was the ultimate American fashion designer of the 1970s. His designs were streamlined, adaptable, imaginative, and classic and contemporary at the same time. Lauren's line of women's clothes, which were fashionable and comfortable, borrowed heavily from his menswear line. In 1977, actress Diane Keaton popularized this look in the movie *Annie Hall*. The following year, believing the cowboy look represented confidence and independence, Lauren introduced a western theme into his clothes. It was an instant sensation. For his work, Lauren received six prestigious Coty awards, more than any other designer. *Photo reproduced by permission of Hulton/Archive.*

Phyllis Schlafly (1924–) Phyllis Schlafly was an effective conservative Republican spokesperson in the 1970s. Arguing that social changes jeopardized the family and traditional gender roles, Schlafly strongly opposed the women's liberation movement. To that end, she organized and operated the National Committee to Stop the ERA as well as the Eagle Forum. Through these organizations, Schlafly and other like-minded conservatives were able to convince voters and legislators that the Equal Rights Amendment (ERA) was a threat to American values, and the amendment was eventually defeated. *Photo reproduced by permission of AP/Wide World Photos.*

WOMEN'S LIBERATION

Women's liberation (variously referred to as feminism or the women's rights movement) was to the 1970s what the civil rights movement was to the 1960s: the most significant social movement in the United States. The two movements shared many similarities: Both were controversial, had many opponents, and resulted in far-reaching and lasting political and social effects. Although feminism successfully sought social opportunities previously denied to women, not all women benefited. In fact, feminism negatively affected some women. In general, however, the movement improved the economic status and freedom of most women, but they still had a long way to go to achieve social equality.

One of feminism's most significant demands was gender equity in wages: equal pay for equal work. In the 1970s, increasing numbers of young women rejected the traditional role of suburban housewife, entering the workplace instead. The economic downturn in the decade forced women as well as men to seek sources of income. As a result, many older women, some of whom had never worked outside the home before, were pressured to work alongside their daughters in factories and offices.

Yet neither the young female activists nor their mothers were paid as well as their male counterparts. On average, they earned just 57 percent of the wages paid to men. Women were shortchanged further by labor laws passed at the beginning of the twentieth century that prevented women from working overtime. Moreover, like African Americans and other minorities, women often were forced to work the lowest-paid, most menial jobs.

Title VII of the Civil Rights Act of 1964 had made job discrimination illegal. Yet the federal government agency created to enforce this law, the Equal Employment Opportunity Commission (EEOC), failed to act on behalf of women for most of the 1960s, instead focusing on minorities. Under pressure from women activists at the beginning of the 1970s, the EEOC finally began to help women workers, by filing gender discrimination lawsuits against companies. Occupational barriers against women began to fall. The U.S. Congress passed additional legislation prohibiting sex discrimination, and it also granted a tax deduction for childcare expenses in families where both parents worked. For the first time, women were admitted to military academies and Ivy League universities. By 1974, Nevada was the only state that had retained its laws limiting overtime work for women.

Although more women gained access to the workplace and its benefits, they still were not paid as much as men. And many professional women complained that regardless of their credentials or achievements, high-paying, high-prestige jobs were denied to them. Feminists believed fair employment laws alone were not enough to elevate their social status, so they sought other laws and changes. They faced strong opposition, some of it from fellow women.

Battles between feminists and their opponents reached a fevered pitch over two main issues: the Equal Rights Amendment (ERA; see box on page 106) and abortion. In 1972, the U.S. Congress passed the ERA, which stated that "equality of rights under the law shall not be denied or abridged by the United States or by any State on account of sex." Before this simply worded amendment could become part of the U.S. Constitution, thirty-eight states had to ratify it by 1979. Twenty-five states quickly approved the amendment, but organized opposition soon stalled the approval process. Led by Phyllis Schlafly and other conservatives, opponents argued that the ERA would bring sweeping social changes that would radically affect marriage, divorce, child custody, adoption, and

Equal rights activists celebrate outside the U.S. Capitol after the Senate extended the ratification period for the Equal Rights Amendment in 1978. **Reproduced by permission of the Corbis Corporation.**

Equal Rights Amendment

The U.S. Congress first considered an Equal Rights Amendment (ERA) in 1923, three years after women were given the constitutional right to vote in the United States. Each year thereafter, the amendment proposal was introduced into each session of Congress but was never passed. In 1971, the proposed amendment was modified, calling for men and women to be given equal treatment under the law. This new version was approved in the U.S. House of Representatives by a vote of 354 to 24. The following year, by a vote of 84 to 8, the U.S. Senate overwhelmingly voted in favor of the amendment. It was then sent to the legislatures of all fifty states for ratification. To become part of the U.S. Constitution, the ERA had be approved by the legislatures of three-fourths of the states (thirty-eight states total) within seven years.

By early 1973, twenty-five states had ratified the ERA. Then its progress slowed dramatically. By 1977, only ten more states had ratified the ERA, three short of the number needed for adoption. In 1978, proponents of the amendment successfully lobbied the U.S. Congress to extend the deadline for ratification from 1979 to 1982. However, no state ratified the ERA after 1977, and three states tried to rescind or take back their original ratification votes. In 1982, the ERA's deadline passed and the amendment was defeated.

What happened? The majority of Americans, both women and men, supported the ERA. However, for a constitutional amendment to be ratified, it

other areas of American family life. Such arguments were effective, raising the fear in the minds of many Americans that social change was proceeding too quickly in the country. By the end of the decade, the ERA failed to gain enough support for approval, and it disappeared from the political landscape.

In the landmark 1973 *Roe* v. *Wade* case, the U.S. Supreme Court ruled that a woman, as part of her constitutional right to privacy, may choose to have an abortion within the first three months of her pregnancy. The ruling divided the nation: Conservatives and religious groups denounced the decision, claiming that abortion was murder. They further felt that legalized abortion would undermine the family, allowing women to use abortion as a type of birth control. On the other hand, feminists and many oth-

must have the support of a majority of legislators in each of the required thirty-eight states. That means the amendment must have broad support and little opposition. The opposition to the ERA, while initially a small minority, was extremely vocal in emphasizing several key issues that ultimately stopped ratification.

Leading the fight against the ERA was Phyllis Schlafly, a longtime conservative activist. In 1972, shortly after the U.S. Senate had passed the amendment, she had organized the National Committee to Stop the ERA. Schlafly and others who joined her cause believed the ERA, as it was written, was so vague and open-ended that it would lead to sweeping changes in American social life that would destroy families. They believed it would, among other things, lead to a loss of alimony for women in divorce cases, the drafting of women into the military, and the creation of unisex, or single-sex, bathrooms. Schlafly also seized upon the issue of states' rights, telling state legislators that the amendment would transfer state power to the federal government.

While many people thought these claims were exaggerated, enough people believed the claims to voice their concerns. This was especially true in conservative southern states. In the end, the fear of social change, real or imagined, was too much for a number of Americans, and the ERA stalled until it died.

ers supported the ruling, asserting it was central to a new role for women in American society. Women, they insisted, have the intellectual capacity and emotional compassion to determine whether to end their pregnancy. This profound difference of opinion continued throughout the 1970s and the following decades.

Beyond the disagreements, feminism achieved several breakthroughs in employment opportunities and social status for women in the 1970s. President Richard M. Nixon (1913–1994) appointed the first two women military generals in 1970. Two years later, the Federal Bureau of Investigation (FBI) hired its first female agent. Throughout the decade, women flooded into previously male-dominated professions. For example, female student enrollment increased dramatically in law and medical schools across the country. Women not only increased their numbers in state and federal legislatures, but they also became influential politicians. Women's strength, intelligence, and grace affected all facets of American society, from sports to academia to the media.

Despite these achievements, there was a dark side to the women's movement. Working-class women were often hurt by the very reforms feminists sought. For example, divorce laws, made simpler to increase the options available to unhappy women, benefited wealthy women the most. Less financially secure women were abandoned by their husbands, who took advantage of the new, quick, no-fault divorce laws leaving their wives without alimony and often with children. These women, unprepared for the workplace, often had to settle for low-paying jobs, and they soon joined the ranks of the working poor. Even those women who could earn higher wages still had to struggle to raise their children, maintain their household, and hold their job. For decades, women have had to struggle for an equal voice in American society, and that struggle did not end in the 1970s.

SOCIAL JUSTICE: ETHNIC PRIDE AND GAY LIBERATION

Women were not alone in their fight for social recognition in the 1970s. African Americans, Native Americans, and Hispanic Americans each formed their own powerful social movement: Black Pride, American Indian Movement (AIM), and Brown Power, respectively. Members of these movements sought ethnic pride and social reform, at times using violent tactics, in a society they felt was ruled by Anglo-Saxon or "white" culture. Indeed, a wave of group consciousness among members of minority ethnic and racial groups swept the country during the decade. A related, but no less important, social-justice movement was the gay liberation movement, which strove to end discrimination in American society on the basis of sexual orientation.

For African Americans, the aim of the Civil Rights movement of the 1960s was social equality. The aim of the Black Pride movement of the late 1960s and early 1970s, however, was social identity. Rejecting mainstream standards of beauty, art, and culture, African Americans tried to reclaim their African heritage. They donned dashikis and West African cotton print dresses and scarves, and they wore their hair in an Afro, or "natural," style. This growing pride in the African American community was displayed on popular television shows such as *Sanford and Son* (1972–1977) and *Good Times* (1974–1979). Yet nothing helped better express the reason for African American ethnic pride than the January 1977 miniseries *Roots*. Based on the novel of the same name by Alex Haley, the series, which told the story of Haley's West African ancestors, enthralled viewers of every ethnic background.

Perhaps no ethnic group suffered a greater plight in American society at the beginning of the 1970s than Native Americans. Forty percent were unemployed; ninety percent lived in substandard housing on federal reservations with few benefits of modern life or economic development. Tuberculosis, alcoholism, and suicide marked the lives of many Native Americans. To bring attention to this alarming situation, the American Indian Movement (AIM), a militant Native American group, seized Alcatraz Island (a former U.S. penitentiary) in San Francisco Bay during November 1969. For the next nineteen months, members of AIM occupied the island, protesting Native American living conditions and treaty violations by the U.S. government. The peaceful occupation made the American public aware of the Native Americans' position.

As the movement progressed, demonstrations took on a more serious and often violent tone. In 1973, at the Pine Ridge Reservation at Wounded Knee, South Dakota (site of a massacre of Native Americans by the U.S. Army in 1890), a dispute arose over the tribal chairman, Richard Wilson. Some tribe members felt Wilson was controlled by the U.S. Bureau of Indian Affairs and wanted to impeach him. Tensions escalated and both sides soon armed themselves for a siege that lasted ten weeks before a peaceful conclusion was reached. Federal law enforcement officials, the Bureau of Indian Affairs, and the national news media all had become involved in the ordeal known as "Wounded Knee II."

The militance of AIM sparked a decade's worth of change for Native Americans. In 1974, the U.S. Congress passed the Indian Self-Determination Act, giving Native Americans the right to control federal and educational aid on their reservations. Throughout the decade, Native Americans also challenged in court the legality of treaties with the U.S. government. Often victorious, they were awarded millions of dollars for lands illegally seized by the government over the previous two centuries.

Hispanic Americans, concentrated primarily in southwestern U.S. states and cities, were often limited to low-paying, menial jobs in which they were treated with contempt by their employers. Initially organized to seek better working conditions and higher wages for Hispanics, the Brown Power movement soon promoted social reform and ethnic pride in being Chicano. ("Chicano" comes from *Mechicano,* the same Nahuatl, or ancient Aztec, word from which the country of Mexico derived its name.) Spanish-language newspapers and Hispanic television stations cultivated ethnic consciousness. A Chicano renaissance emerged in arts such as theater, literature, and painting. Even network television recognized the blossoming Hispanic pride with a breakthrough sitcom on life in the East Los Angeles barrio, *Chico and the Man* (1974–1978).

Gray Panthers

Maggie Kuhn and five of her friends met in 1970 to discuss social issues relevant to them. Kuhn, then sixty-five years old, was concerned about the problems facing retirees and the elderly, and her friends shared that concern. They decided to form a group called the Consultation of Older and Younger Adults for Social Change in hopes of changing government policies and public attitudes regarding the elderly.

More Americans were getting older in the 1970s. Life expectancy in the United States rose to 69.5 years for white men and 77.2 years for white women. The American population over 65 years of age increased 20 percent in the decade, and twelve million people joined the American Association of Retired Persons (AARP), the nation's leading organization for people aged 50 and older.

Within a few years, Kuhn's group, renamed the Gray Panthers because of their action-oriented and often controversial manner, had over one hundred members divided among eleven chapters. In 1975, the group held its first national convention in Chicago. Continuing to grow and making their demands known through sit-ins, picket lines, and other vocal demonstrations, the Gray Panthers began to effect change. In 1978, the U.S. Congress passed laws to end age discrimination and to increase the age of mandatory retirement from sixty-five to seventy.

The 1970s was a decade of heightened ethnic identity for many other nationalities as well—Jewish Americans, Italian Americans, Irish Americans, Asian Americans. Almost every immigrant group in the United States celebrated its ethnic background with parades, political organizations, and artistic and cultural productions.

As awareness and acceptance of the multiculturalism of America spread across the country, gays and lesbians demanded increased tolerance also. In June 1969, New York City police raided the Stonewall Inn, a gay nightclub, and a riot between police and the patrons of the club ensued. The Stonewall rebellion triggered the gay liberation movement that would continue for decades. Hundreds of gay rights' organizations sprang up in American cities, demanding legal reform, access to public services, and an end to discrimination. To bring about social reform, many gay candidates began to run for public office. Although gays and lesbians did not find widespread public acceptance at first, their fight helped promote a new mood of tolerance in the United States.

THE RISE OF NEOCONSERVATISM AND TELEVANGELISM

As differences in culture and sexual orientation were acknowledged and accepted in American society during the 1970s, some rebels, mostly members of the baby boom generation, pushed for an even greater acceptance of alternative lifestyles. The baby boomers, born after World War II between 1946 and 1964, represented the largest segment of the population and thus had significant influence on social trends. The youth culture of the 1960s, known as the counterculture, continued to flourish in the 1970s. Young people rejected capitalism, competition, social conventions, and the work ethic of their parents. They embraced cooperation, toleration, and freedom of expression.

In contrast to their parents' belief in monogamy (one sexual partner within marriage), young people championed sexual experimentation. An

Two armed Native Americans stand guard with rifles during the ordeal that became known as "Wounded Knee II." **Reproduced by permission of the Corbis Corporation.**

outgrowth of this was the so-called sexual revolution of the 1970s. During the decade, many young people cast aside traditional sexual restraints, ignoring many former sexual taboos: interracial dating, open homosexuality, communal living, casual nudity, and lewd language. In part because of the development of the birth-control pill and other contraceptives, sexual activity increased among the young. Sensuality and sexuality became a significant part of fashion, movies, rock music, and popular novels. Pornography became big business.

The counterculture and its revolutions in lifestyle, sexual standards, and family life alarmed not only conservatives but also some liberals. Disillusioned with the political and social changes around them, former liberal Democrats such as Daniel Patrick Moynihan and Jeanne Kirkpatrick became spokespersons for a social trend known as neoconservatism. They broke with their former political allies over what they perceived as a rising anti-American sentiment sweeping the country in the wake of the Vietnam War (1954–75). Neoconservatives questioned the expansion of welfare and other governmental programs they believed were putting a strain on the nation's economic productivity during a recession.

Neoconservatives also railed against what they asserted were radical reforms that had destroyed moral virtues in American society, in areas ranging from education to religion. With their concerns about contemporary social trends, neoconservatives found powerful allies in the fundamentalist Protestant churches that became politically active in the 1970s. Like neoconservatives, fundamentalist Christians reacted against the turmoil of the 1960s. Often called born-again Christians, they opposed the liberal influences and secularism (belief that religion should have no part in political or civic affairs) they felt were destroying American values.

Fundamentalists represented just one aspect of the growing emphasis on religion and spirituality felt by many Americans in the 1970s. At the beginning of the decade, a Gallup poll found that only 4 percent of Americans felt religion was important in their lives. By 1976, however, that number had risen to 44 percent. Seizing upon the growing born-again Christian movement across America, especially in the South and West, preachers took to the airwaves to spread their message. These television evangelists, or televangelists, included Jimmy Swaggert, Oral Roberts, Jim and Tammy Bakker, Billy Graham, and Jerry Falwell. Combined, they had an estimated weekly audience of twenty-four million viewers who tuned into their religious talk shows and contributed millions of dollars each year to their crusades.

In 1979, Jerry Falwell turned his religious crusade into a political one when he organized the Moral Majority. Opposing abortion, homosexuality, pornography, and the Equal Rights Amendment, this group lobbied for

Studio 54

Studio 54 was a Manhattan discotheque that was, for a few brief years, the hottest nightclub on the planet. Steve Rubell and Ian Shrager opened the dance club in 1977 in a run-down warehouse that formerly housed a television studio. Designed to appeal to the hip and trendy "beautiful people" bored by ordinary discotheques, Studio 54 admitted only a select few people deemed glamorous enough for entry. Outside, large crowds of wanna-bes stood in line for hours for a chance to be admitted or to see movie stars, famous athletes, or political celebrities. A huge success, the club earned an estimated seven million dollars in its first year.

laws reflecting what they defined as conservative Christian values. The four million members of the Moral Majority advocated prayer and the teaching of creationism (the belief that the Bible's account of Creation is literally true) in schools and an increase in military spending by the federal government. This special-interest group exerted great influence on neoconservatives and the Republican Party, helping to shape the political landscape in the decades that followed.

THE "ME DECADE" AND THE SEARCH FOR NEW RELIGIONS

Although far more Americans cited religion as an important part of their lives in the 1970s than in previous decades, not all turned to Christianity and its various forms. Whereas Americans in the 1960s had been preoccupied with questions of social and political justice, Americans in the 1970s were concerned with self-fulfillment and personal happiness. For many, "religion" came in the form of self-therapy and psychological analysis. Almost everyone seemed to have an analyst, guru, genie, prophet, priest, or spirit guide. Writing in *New York* magazine in August 1976, novelist Tom Wolfe coined the term "Me Decade" to describe Americans' preoccupation with themselves in the 1970s.

Unable or unwilling to solve social problems, Americans focused on satisfying their own desires through health food, diets, hot tubs, and physical exercise. Many young Americans took up kung fu, aikido, yoga, tennis, jogging, massage, camping, hiking, skiing, and dancing, among other physical activities. It was a decade to "do your own thing."

We Were Kung Fu Fighting

Martial artist and actor Bruce Lee's 1972 martial-arts film *Fists of Fury* and his 1973 follow-up, *Enter the Dragon,* started an American obsession with kung fu and other Asian martial arts. As with many other crazes or fads, no is quite sure why it caught on. Whatever the reason, it was extremely popular: Almost every American city and suburb boasted a storefront gym where karate, kung fu, judo, jujitsu, aikido, or some other form of Asian fighting was taught.

The American media quickly seized on the fad. On the silver screen, actors such as Bruce Lee, Tom Laughlin, and Chuck Norris were featured in kick-boxing epics. On television, the weekly western *Kung Fu* began airing in the fall of 1972. In the series, Shaolin priest Kwai Chang Caine, played by actor David Carradine, wandered the American West in the nineteenth century looking for his half-brother, while subduing his opponents and offering snippets of Buddhist wisdom. And on the pop music charts, Carl Douglas's *Kung Fu Fighting* reached number one in the fall of 1974. Although the craze for martial arts gradually cooled by the end of the decade, the Asian disciplines have remained a permanent feature of American pop culture.

More significant, the "Me Decade" reflected a sense of spiritual crisis. The counterculture had rejected traditional religion as meaningless and corrupt, so many Americans turned to Eastern religions such as Zen Buddhism and Hinduism. Still others became disciples of various mystics and preachers whose teachings offered the promise of inner peace and enlightenment. Indian mystic Maharishi Mahesh Yogi introduced a mantra-chanting system called transcendental meditation (TM) that promised practitioners a relaxed physical and mental state. Indian swami A.C. Bhaktivedanta founded a religious movement known as Hare Krishna. The cotton-robed followers of the movement, who worshiped the Hindu god Krishna, were most often visible on street corners or in airports, where they enthusiastically solicited funds for their group.

Perhaps the largest of these alternative religions was the Unification Church. Founded by Sun Myung Moon, a South Korean industrialist, the Unification Church was a fusion of Asian philosophy, Christianity, and capitalism. Moon claimed to be the new messiah who would unite all the religions of the world and reinterpret the Bible. Although his missionaries

Organic Foods

With the spread of the environmental movement across the country in the 1970s came a rising interest in organic, or naturally produced, foods. What started out as a fad at the beginning of the decade soon became a staple of mainstream American culture. Concerned consumers wanted a diet that was healthy, not only for them but also for the planet. Food products produced with artificial pesticides, fertilizers, feed additives, and growth regulators were shunned in favor of those produced using such Earth-friendly farming techniques as biological pest control and crop rotation. Chemical preservatives, food additives, sugar, salt, and white flour were also avoided by the health-conscious. *Natural, biodegradable,* and *organic* were the new buzzwords for informed consumers who demanded that supermarkets stock natural foods. By the mid-1970s, items such as tofu, brown rice, lentils, sprouts, and whole-grain bread could be found on ordinary supermarket shelves.

(called Moonies) had been in the United States since 1960, Moon did not attract widespread attention until he transferred his headquarters to New York City and preached to twenty thousand people at Madison Square Garden in September 1974. Like Krishnas, young Moonies became increasingly visible on street corners, preaching Moon's beliefs and collecting money for the church. By the end of the decade, Moon and his church came under heavy criticism for allegedly brainwashing his young followers and making controversial financial deals.

The rising interest in religious cults like the Moonies in the United States during the 1970s was mirrored by a rising interest in the occult. Americans became increasingly interested in mysticism and parapsychology as a means to explain the nature of things. They explored satanism, witchcraft, astrology, tarot cards, the Bermuda Triangle, the lost island of Atlantis, unidentified flying objects (UFOs), and extrasensory perception (ESP).

Many Americans soon became alarmed at the popularity of religious cults, however, fearing for the safety of followers of self-described prophets and messiahs. That fear was realized tragically in the Jonestown massacre that occurred on November 18, 1978. In the mid-1950s, James

("Jim") Warren Jones had established the People's Temple, a Christian-based congregation. After moving his group to California in 1965, Jones began to adopt increasingly radical political and religious beliefs. Among other claims, he told his followers he was God. In 1977, following allegations of financial misconduct, Jones persuaded his congregation to relocate to Jonestown, Guyana. Amid reports of physical and psychological torture at Jonestown, U.S. Congressman Leo Ryan of California flew to Guyana with a group of journalists and others to investigate the charges in November 1978. When the congressman and his group tried to leave the colony on November 14, they were shot and killed by cult members. Four days later, Jones presided over an enforced suicide ceremony during which all 913 of his followers drank Kool-Aid laced with cyanide. Jones died later that day from a gunshot wound, possibly self-inflicted.

FASHION: DO YOUR OWN THING

Fashions in the 1970s reflected the social attitude of the decade: traditionalism was out, self-expression was in. Choice, personality, and comfort were the fashion hallmarks of the 1970s for women. For men, work wear was replaced by sportswear; leisure was the key. And for youth, the only fashion was antifashion.

American women benefited enormously from the fashion innovations of the 1960s. In the wake of such fashion breakthroughs as psychedelic colors, miniskirts, and pants, American women had a new range of looks from which to choose. They were no longer willing to follow the lead of fashion designers, and they broke down traditional categories in fashion. The "do your own thing" attitude in clothes emphasized a woman's personality, her independence of mind, and her spirit of experimentation.

Hot pants, short shorts for women, burst onto the scene in 1971 to rival the still-popular miniskirt. New variations in pants appeared in long and short culottes that hung like a skirt, harem pants that bloused at the ankle, and knickers worn with boots. Most important, women felt free to wear a wide range of clothes to work, from pantsuits to casual sweater sets to knee-length or mid-calf-length dresses. Also popular were flowing pants, short jackets, and peasant-style blouses and skirts. It did not matter what a woman wore, as long as she could create her own comfortable style and look.

Designers quickly caught on, offering casual-dress options for women. Collections of interchangeable separates allowed a woman to create her own look that was suitable for day and evening wear. When women opted to dress in traditional men's clothes, designers responded, giving them plenty of male styles from which to choose.

For men, the most important fashion innovations in the 1970s were the increase in leisure wear and the use of new colors and fabrics. The white shirt and dark suit, the standard attire for men at work, virtually disappeared. Replacing it were double-knit and stretch-knit leisure suits in bold colors such as rose, purple, orange, and green. Wide ties in big floral prints and brightly patterned synthetic shirts often completed the look.

Throughout the decade, more and more men unbuttoned their shirts, going without ties and often without jackets. This new ethic of leisure and individuality emphasized lifestyle over work, and the lifestyle of choice was fun and relaxation. Sportswear, a category of clothing that had been growing since the 1950s, exploded in the 1970s. Unstructured jackets were worn over vests or sweaters. Rugged sportswear, once worn for hunting, fishing, or ski trips, made its way into men's weekend wear. The most popular outfit was the jogging suit, worn by joggers and non-joggers alike. It became fashionable to look like an athlete.

Young Americans, both women and men, rejected the dictates of the fashion industry, turning instead to unisex, carefree dress and hairstyles.

The bodies of People's Temple cult members lie on the ground in Jonestown, Guyana, after cult leader Jim Jones persuaded them to participate in a mass suicide by drinking Kool-Aid laced with cyanide. **Reproduced by permission of the Corbis Corporation.**

Faded denim jeans or army fatigues, cotton T-shirts or sleeveless tank tops, and boots outfitted youth of the 1970s. College students of both sexes continued to wear their hair long. The shag cut, short on top, longer on the sides, and flat in back, was one of the first haircuts to be popular with both men and women. A popular women's hairstyle, inspired by 1976 Olympic gold medalist figure skater Dorothy Hamill, was the short, layered wedge.

Many young women and men shopped at secondhand clothing stores and army/navy outlets. They blended old and new looks to forge a distinct counterculture style: an antique shirt with dirty blue jeans and a beret, or an Indian tunic with army fatigues. Cotton and other natural fabrics were chosen over knit blends and polyester. Self-defined fashion, not the fashion of their parents, was the uniform of American youth in the 1970s.

One new garment that captured the fancy of Americans in the decade, regardless of gender or age, was designer jeans. In the 1960s and early 1970s, a pair of dirty, torn blue jeans was the universal clothing item, especially for people under twenty-five—the antifashion statement of a generation. Deciding to capitalize on this phenomenon, designers like

A group of young men dressed in typical 1970s fashion. ©Lynn Goldsmith. Reproduced by permission of the Corbis Corporation.

Calvin Klein redesigned and repackaged jeans into a high-fashion item adorned with embroidered logos, rhinestones, and silver studs. Despite selling for three and four times the cost of ordinary jeans, designer jeans quickly became a fixture in the American jeans market.

For More Information

BOOKS

Bolden, Tonya, ed. *33 Things Every Girl Should Know About Women's History: From Suffragettes to Skirt Lengths to the ERA.* New York: Crown Publications, 2002.

Ferriss, Susan, and Ricardo Sandoval. *The Fight in the Fields: Cesar Chavez and the Farmworkers Movement.* New York: Harvest Books, 1998.

Deangelis, Gina. *Jonestown Massacre: Tragic End of a Cult.* Berkeley Heights, NJ: Enslow, 2002.

Haley, Alex. *Roots: The Saga of an American Family.* New York: Dell, 1980.

Hearst, Patricia Campbell, and Alvin Moscow. *Every Secret Thing.* Garden City, NY: Doubleday, 1982.

Matthiessen, Peter. *In the Spirit of Crazy Horse.* Reprint ed. New York: Penguin, 1992.

Schulman, Bruce J. *The Seventies: The Great Shift in American Culture, Society, and Politics.* New York: Free Press, 2001.

WEB SITES

American Indian Movement. http://www.aimovement.org/ (accessed on February 27, 2002).

Clothing Fashions of the 1970s. http://www.geocities.com/gertrudegerty/cloth.html (accessed on February 27, 2002).

Neoconservatism Online. http://www.neoconservatism.com/ (accessed on February 27, 2002).

Women's Liberation Movement. http://www.britannica.com/women/articles/women's_liberation_movement.html (accessed on February 27, 2002).

Yesterdayland–Fashion from the 70s. http://www.yesterdayland.com/popopedia/shows/decades/fashion_1970s.php (accessed on February 27, 2002).

chapter six

Medicine and Health

1970: The U.S. Congress passes the Occupational Safety and Health Act to ensure worker and workplace safety.

1970: **July 23** The nutritional content of breakfast cereals comes under fire before the U.S. Senate Commerce Committee.

1970: **December 30** The U.S. Congress passes the Poison Prevention Packaging Act, requiring manufacturers of potentially dangerous products to put safety tops on their containers so children will not be able to open them. The law takes effect in 1972.

1971: **January 1** Cigarette advertising on U.S. radio and television is banned.

1971: **March 18** Soft contact lenses win the approval of the U.S. Food and Drug Administration.

1971: **December 24** President Richard M. Nixon signs the National Cancer Act, authorizing the allocation of $1.5 billion per year to combat the nation's second-leading cause of death.

1972: The National Academy of Sciences suggests that air pollution probably explains why cancer rates are twice as high in cities as in rural areas.

1972: **January 10** The U.S. Surgeon General's report on smoking warns that nonsmokers exposed to cigarette smoke may suffer health risks.

1973: The American Psychiatric Association removes homosexuality from its list of mental illnesses, redefining it as a "sexual orientation disturbance."

1973: The U.S. Congress passes the HMO Act, regulating health maintenance organizations.

1973: **January 22** The U.S. Supreme Court's *Roe V. Wade* decision provides women with a constitutional guarantee of abortion rights.

1974: The computerized axial tomography (CAT) scanner gains widespread use.

1974: **June** The Heimlich manuever is introduced as first aid for choking victims.

1974: **August 12** President Gerald R. Ford urges Congress to pass national health insurance legislation.

1975: Lyme disease, a disease transmitted by ticks to humans, is identified in Lyme, Connecticut.

1975: The first U.S. strike by doctors is carried out in New York City hospitals.

1975: **May** California doctors organize a month-long strike to protest rising insurance costs and inefficiencies in health care.

1976: The U.S. General Accounting Office reports a startling program of sterilization of thousands of Native American women without their consent by the Indian Health Service.

1976: Karen Ann Quinlan's parents win a court battle to turn off the respirator keeping their comatose daughter alive.

1976: An outbreak of Legionnaires' disease occurs at the Philadelphia convention of the American Legion. Twenty-nine people die.

1976: A swine-flu epidemic threatens to sweep the United States. Millions are vaccinated, but the warning turns out to be a false alarm.

1977: U.S. scientists identify the previously unknown bacterium responsible for causing Legionnaires' disease.

1977: **July 2** The first magnetic resonance imaging (MRI) scanner is tested.

1977: **October 26** The world's last known case of smallpox is reported in Somalia. Two years later, the World Health Organization will announce that the disease has been eradicated.

1978: **January 11** The secretary of the U.S. Health, Education, and Welfare department calls cigarette smoking "slow-motion suicide."

1978: **February 17** The U.S. Food and Drug Administration issues the first federal mandatory safety performance standard for equipment producing ultrasonic radiation used in physical-therapy treatments.

1978: **July 25** The world's first test-tube baby is born in London, England.

1979: **February 11** The Commerce Department reports that U.S. cigarette manufacturers continue to increase sales despite cancer warnings.

1979: **March 19** The American Heart Association says moderate consumption of alcoholic beverages may protect against death from heart disease.

1979: **November 18** The Centers for Disease Control reports that the incidence of gonorrhea has leveled off, but cases of syphilis, a far more serious venereal disease, are increasing.

Overview

Health care was a critical concern in America in the 1970s. Although the medical and health industries grew rapidly during the decade to become second only to the military in size and cost, many Americans still lacked access to basic health care. Technological advances in other industries made their way into the medical field, resulting in revolutionary devices such as computerized axial tomography (CAT) and magnetic resonance imaging (MRI) scanners. These and other scientific breakthroughs helped improve medical care and extended the lives of many people.

But these advances also raised philosophical issues of life and death, including ethical dilemmas regarding quality of life. The tragic case of Karen Ann Quinlan forced the medical community, the legal system, and average Americans to debate this issue openly for the first time. Like the contentious issue of abortion, also legally addressed in the 1970s, advocates on both sides of the right-to-die issue believed their views were morally correct.

As medical issues increasingly made headlines in the decade, people began to exercise to improve their own health. From bicycling to yoga, on dirt paths and in fancy health clubs, people across the country joined in what became known as the fitness movement. Jogging or running was the exercise of choice for millions of Americans, and women became as active as men in the pursuit of personal health and well-being.

Despite this movement, traditional health problems—heart disease, cancer, and stroke—continued to plague many Americans, and health care costs were skyrocketing. Seeking to stem those rising costs and make health care more affordable, the federal government enacted laws to help develop prepaid, group health plans called health maintenance organizations, or HMOs. These plans, in which subscribers paid a set monthly fee for basic medical services, marked a big change from the old fee-for-service arrangement under which a patient paid for each separate visit and service at a doctor's office.

Medical researchers in governmental agencies also worked with other scientists to identify and combat previously unknown viruses that had the potential to threaten large segments of American society. Lyme disease and Legionnaires' disease were two new diseases addressed successfully by timely and effective government response. But the government could also act blindly, perceiving a health threat that never emerged. This was the case with swine flu, and many people died because of the error.

Kenneth C. Edelin (1937–) Kenneth C. Edelin, chief resident in obstetrics at Boston City Hospital, was found guilty of manslaughter on February 15, 1975, and sentenced to one year's probation. Prosecutors had accused him of killing a male fetus after he had performed a legal abortion at the hospital on October 3, 1973. The seventeen-year-old mother had been in her twentieth to twenty-second week of pregnancy. Prosecutors had argued that the fetus had been old enough to be considered a living being; Edelin's lawyers had argued otherwise. On December 17, 1976, the Massachusetts Supreme Court overturned Edelin's conviction. *Photo reproduced by permission of AP/Wide World Photos.*

James F. Fixx (1932–1984) James F. Fixx was an overweight magazine editor who started running in 1969 to improve his conditioning. That decision changed not only his life but also the lives of many others. In 1977, he published *The Complete Book of Running*. The best-selling book helped spur Americans to pursue running as a means to better health. By the end of the 1970s, one hundred thousand people were finishing marathons each year. An estimated nine million Americans ran at least one hundred days a year. *Photo reproduced by permission of the Corbis Corporation.*

Donald A. Henderson (1928–) Donald A. Henderson, director of the World Health Organization's program to eradicate smallpox, accepted the Albert Lasker Public Service Award in 1976 on behalf of the organization. Under Henderson's direction, massive vaccination programs had been initiated around the world to rid the planet of this dreaded disease. In late 1979, smallpox was officially certified as eradicated. The virus, however, is not extinct: Samples of the organism continue to survive in two laboratories in the United States and Russia.

Rosalyn S. Yalow (1921–) Rosalyn S. Yalow became the second woman ever to win the Nobel Prize in Physiology or Medicine when she was given the award in 1977. A medical physicist, Yalow was honored for developing, in collaboration with her associate Soloman A. Berson, the laboratory procedure called radioimmunoassay (RIA). Scientists use RIA to measure the concentration of hundreds of chemical and biological substances in the blood and other fluids of the human body. Yalow had invented the technique in 1959 initially to measure the amount of insulin in the blood of adult diabetics. *Photo courtesy of the Library of Congress.*

KAREN ANN QUINLAN AND THE RIGHT TO DIE

On the night of April 15, 1975, while at a friend's birthday party, Karen Ann Quinlan drank several gin-and-tonics and swallowed at least one tranquilizer. The combination of alcohol and drugs had a disastrous effect on the twenty-one-year-old. When she collapsed and stopped breathing, her friends called the police. By the time she was rushed to nearby Newton Memorial Hospital in New Jersey, she had ceased to breathe for at least two separate fifteen-minute periods.

Quinlan's parents arrived at the hospital to find her in a coma. The attending physicians believed her brain had been damaged irreversibly, although they did not know exactly why she had stopped breathing. They described her condition as a persistent vegetative state, which meant she had some brain activity, but was permanently unconscious and was not aware of herself or her surroundings. Physicians performed a tracheotomy to help her breathe, cutting a hole in her throat and inserted a respirating tube into her trachea. They also inserted a tube through her nose that supplied water and artificial nutrition to her stomach.

Within days of her admission to the hospital, Quinlan began to assume a fetal position. As the damage to her brain progressed, her physicians held out no hope for her recovery. On April 24, she was transferred to St. Claire's Hospital in Danville, New Jersey, and was placed in the intensive care unit. After three months, with her condition steadily deteriorating, Quinlan's parents met with her attending physicians and the hospital chaplain. All agreed that her respirator should be removed. Her father then signed a release asking the hospital to do so.

Yet a few days later, with the support of the hospital, Quinlan's primary physician refused to disconnect her respirator, citing moral concerns. As a physician, he was obligated to save lives. By withdrawing Quinlan's treatment, he believed, he would cause her death.

In response, Quinlan's parents went to court seeking to have her father named her legal guardian, which would give him the right to authorize the decision to disconnect the respirator. New Jersey's attorney general, the county prosecutor, the attending physicians, and the hospital joined together to block such action.

The court was faced with a dilemma. There was no precedent (previous legal case) that addressed such an issue. Traditional legal definitions of death had been complicated by advances in medical technology, which preserved the lives of patients who previously would have died. This life-saving technology raised many questions: Has anyone the legal right to terminate care and condemn a patient to almost-certain death? If so, who has that right? And under what conditions can that right be given? Faced with these questions, the court sided against the Quinlans and appointed someone else to be her legal guardian.

The Quinlan family appealed the decision to the New Jersey Supreme Court. On March 31, 1976, almost a year after Quinlan had slipped into a coma, the state supreme court unanimously overturned the lower court's judgment. In its landmark ruling, the court appointed Quinlan's father her guardian with full legal authority to make decisions about her care. It allowed him to decide to disconnect the life-support system with the agreement of the hospital's ethics committee.

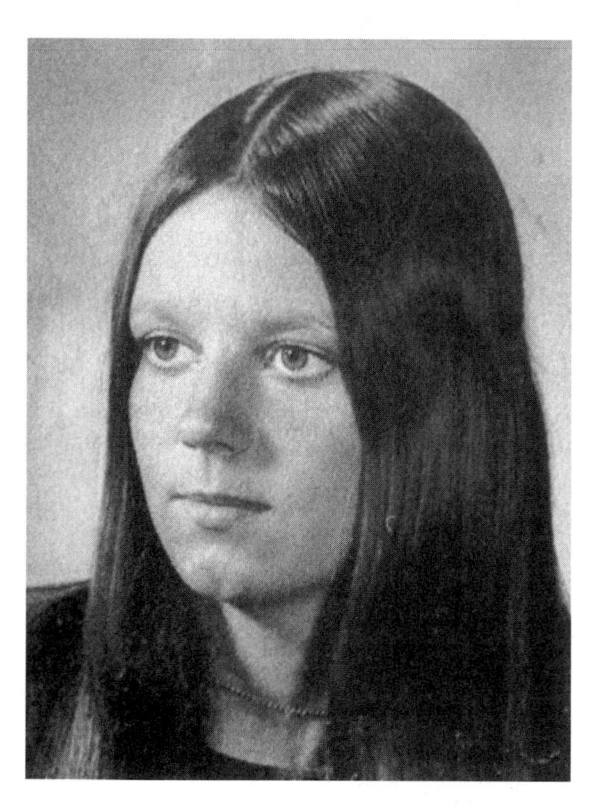

A photo of Karen Ann Quinlan before the 1975 accident that left her in a coma and led to the court battle regarding her family's decision to take her off a respirator. **Reproduced by permission of the Corbis Corporation.**

Ironically, sensing the court would rule in favor of the Quinlans, the hospital medical staff had already begun to wean Quinlan off the respirator so she might be able to breathe on her own. Even after the decision was handed down, the hospital refused to remove the respirator immediately. Finally, in May 1976, Quinlan was taken off the respirator permanently. A month later, her parents transferred her to a nursing home where she remained for the next nine years. She lingered in a coma in a rigid fetal position, breathing on her own and receiving nutrients through a tube in her nose. On June 11, 1985, at the age of thirty-one, Quinlan died of pneumonia.

THE FITNESS MOVEMENT

In 1968, Dallas physician Kenneth Cooper coined the word *aerobics* and published a slim book by the same name that promoted the health benefits of regular, moderate aerobic exercise. Although it ran counter to almost all the conventional medical wisdom at the time, the book spurred a fitness revolution in the 1970s. Aerobics, bicycling, dancing, jogging, isometrics, stretching, swimming, walking, yoga—Americans tried anything to improve their health, flatten their stomachs, cure their bad backs, or reduce their stress levels.

By 1977, a record 87.5 million Americans over the age of eighteen claimed to participate in athletic activities. That same year, James Fixx

New Technologies in Medicine

Advances in military technology, computer technology, and bioengineering (the combination of medicine and engineering) in the 1960s and early 1970s led to a technological revolution in medicine. Of great benefit to patients and medical personnel were newly created devices and techniques such as ultrasound, CAT scanners, MRI, and microsurgery.

Medical researchers borrowed sonar technology from the military and used it to create ultrasound, high- frequency electromagnetic waves that cannot be heard by humans. Like X rays, ultrasound allows physicians to see inside the human body, helping to diagnose problems without resorting to surgery. Ultrasound is an especially helpful tool for monitoring a fetus while it is still in the uterus, or womb.

An imaging device closely related to ultrasound is a computerized axial tomography (CAT) scanner. A CAT scanner is an X-ray machine that rotates around a person's body, recording data images of a specific body part from many different angles. That data is then sent to a computer, which collects it into a three-dimensional image. With little discomfort to a patient, a physician can then make a diagnosis based on the image.

MRI, or magnetic resonance imaging, is a sophisticated diagnostic procedure that allows a physician to view the inside of a patient's body without using X rays. Instead, the MRI scanner uses magnetic fields and radio waves to generate detailed, computerized, three-dimensional images of many different parts of the body, such as organs, bones, joints, and blood vessels. Sensitive to soft tissue, it can also provide detailed images of lesions and tumors.

published *The Complete Book of Running,* a best-seller that motivated some nine million joggers to trot along urban park paths and suburban byways. Thousands of those joggers raised their fitness levels high enough to participate in marathons held around the country. By far, joggers were the most visible sign of the fitness boom.

Although people competed in marathons and other organized events, the new athletics sweeping the country minimized the importance of competition. For many, finishing a race was a victory, regardless of the final position relative to their fellow runners. For others, just participating brought them joy and a sense of accomplishment. And for a few, a solitary early-morning jog on a deserted city street or a bicycle ride on a quiet country road provided physical and mental benefits not available from any traditional sporting activity.

Recreation became fitness and fitness became big business in America in the 1970s. Aerobic dancing, home-conditioning equipment, and enrollment in health clubs fueled a $2-billion-a-year exercise industry. The cost of working out, and the time needed to do it, limited the fitness movement to the middle and upper classes in America. The movement, however, was not limited to men. Inspired by tennis star Billie Jean King's victory over Bobby Riggs in a 1973 tennis match billed as the "Battle of the Sexes," women began to work out in great numbers. With men and women both working out, often together, fitness activity was transformed from a solitary to a social event. In many large cities, the health club or jogging track replaced the singles bar as a place to meet someone of the opposite sex.

Dallas physician Kenneth Cooper (left), jogging here with others, sparked the fitness movement of the 1970s when he published the book titled Aerobics. ***Reproduced by permission of the Corbis Corporation.***

Top Causes of Death in America in 1975

Cause	Number
1. Heart disease	716,215
2. Cancer	365,693
3. Stroke	194,038
4. Accidents	103,030
5. Influenza and pneumonia	55,664
6. Diabetes	35,230
7. Liver disease	31,623
8. Arteriosclerosis	28,887
9. Suicide	27,063
10. Early infant diseases	26,616

Variously labeled a "fad" or "craze" in the 1970s, the fitness movement began to slow down toward the end of the decade, but it did not fade away. In the years since, fitness has become part of the American lifestyle. Physicians and other medical professionals applaud this fact, knowing that regular exercise reduces heart rate and blood pressure, burns unwanted calories, and relieves stress.

THE RISE OF HMOS

The early years of the Great Depression (period of severe economic decline in the United States from 1929 to 1941) saw the emergence of managed health care systems, which are now called health maintenance organizations (HMOs). In these original prepaid medical care systems, people who enrolled paid a predetermined set fee on a regular basis to a physician, who then provided the necessary care under the terms of the system.

In Elk City, Oklahoma, in 1929, physician Michael Shadid organized a cooperative health plan for several hundred farm families, who paid him an agreed-upon fee for his services. That same year, the Los Angeles Department of Water and Power contracted with two physicians to offer a prepaid health care system to its workers and their families.

Doctors' Average Salaries in 1975

Specialty	Salary
Pathology	$138,000
Radiology	$122,000
Orthopedic surgery	$62,410
Obstetrics/Gynecology	$57,500
General surgery	$53,700
Internal medicine	$53,670
Family practice	$48,160
Pediatrics	$43,460
Psychiatry	$39,460
Dentistry	$30,200

In the following years, other companies across the country set up prepaid group practice plans to make health care available to their workers at costs they could afford. A pioneer in this area was businessman Henry Kaiser, who owned steel mills and shipyards on the West Coast. During World War II (1939–45), Kaiser organized comprehensive health services for the tens of thousands of people he employed. After the war, believing he could reorganize medical care to provide millions of Americans with affordable prepaid health coverage, Kaiser opened the Permanente Health Plan to the public. Within ten years, the health plan (renamed Kaiser Permanente) had a growing network of hospitals and clinics and five hundred thousand members.

In the 1960s and early 1970s, technological advances in medicine and governmental programs such as Medicare (health care for the elderly) and Medicaid (health care for the needy) caused health care costs to rise dramatically. Hoping to limit those rising costs and ensure health coverage for those people who lacked it, President Richard M. Nixon (1913–1994) sought to create new prepaid health plans as a way to improve the country's health system. The president asked the U.S. Congress to establish planning grants and loan guarantees for the development of health maintenance organizations or HMOs. In 1973, Congress responded by passing the Health Maintenance Organization Act, which authorized $375 million in federal funds to help develop HMOs and removed legal regulations that might hamper their development.

Shortage of Health Care Providers

At the beginning of the 1970s, only about 275,000 doctors were treating patients in the United States, an average of one doctor for every 740 people. Most of those doctors, and almost all who specialized in a particular field of medicine, practiced in urban areas. The lack of doctors in rural areas was a growing concern. By the end of the decade, however, an increase in the number of medical schools and the number of students enrolled in those schools helped ease that shortage. In 1979, approximately 399,000 physicians practiced medicine across the country, an average of one doctor for every 570 people. The rising number of specialists in relation to the number of general or family practitioners still remained an issue, though. Over the same time period, the number of nurses also increased, from 700,000 to 1,075,000.

An HMO is a prepaid group practice in which a person or that person's employer (or both) pays a single, prearranged monthly fee for a set of basic and supplemental medical services. Physicians work in HMOs for a salary rather than for specific fees. Members of HMOs receive physicians' services, laboratory tests, X rays, and possibly prescription drugs and some other health care services at little or no extra cost. Limited hospital coverage is also provided, but HMOs try to avoid hospitalization and higher medical costs by emphasizing preventive health care. One of the disadvantages of HMOs is that members have to see physicians that are available within the network or organization rather than physicians of their own choice.

In 1970, thirty HMOs operated within the United States. By the end of the decade, more than two hundred HMOs had been established with over nine million people enrolled. Although that number was far below the goal that governmental administrators had originally set, managed care organizations continued to grow throughout the next several decades.

LEGIONNAIRES' DISEASE: A MYSTERIOUS KILLER REVEALED

At the Bellevue-Stratford Hotel in Philadelphia, Pennsylvania, the Pennsylvania chapter of the American Legion held its fifty-eighth annual convention from July 21 to 24, 1976. (The American Legion, chartered by the U.S. Congress in 1919, is a national organization of American war veterans.) Within forty-eight hours of the start of the convention, legionnaires (members of the American Legion) began to exhibit pneumonia-like symptoms: high fever, chest pains, and lung congestion. By the beginning of August, 221 people were infected with the mysterious illness. Seventy-two of those people were not legionnaires but had been at or near the hotel during the convention. Of those infected, thirty-four eventually died.

Physicians and medical researchers were at a loss to explain the illness. Tracking down the culprit quickly became one of the biggest and most intensive medical investigations ever. Newspapers and other media put forth wild speculation regarding the source of the infection, such as conspiracies against American war veterans by communists and pharmaceutical companies, fueling public fears of an epidemic. The press labeled the unknown illness "Legionnaires' disease."

Researchers from the Centers for Disease Control (CDC), the federal government agency responsible for preventing and controlling disease, were called in to investigate the puzzling outbreak. As in other investigations, these "disease detectives" began by asking questions to try to gather as much evidence about the disease as possible: Who are the victims? What sets them apart from those who are not sick? Where were they when they became ill? What were they doing? What did they eat and drink?

CDC researchers questioned the over four thousand legionnaires who had attended the convention and their family members. They also performed autopsies on the bodies of the victims, looking for any biological clues. Finding that all who became ill were probably exposed at the same time and in the same place, researchers turned their attention to the hotel. They collected samples of air, soil, water, and other materials from the hotel and its grounds.

In January 1977, a breakthrough occurred. In the hotel's cooling tower, researchers discovered a previously unidentified bacterium. Tests confirmed that this bacterium, which researchers named *Legionella pneumophilia,* causes an acute respiratory infection similar to serious pneumonia. The cooling tower supplied water to the hotel's air conditioning system, and so the bacterium had been actively pumped into the hotel.

Since this first known outbreak, governments around the world have instituted strict guidelines for cleaning large-scale air conditioning systems. Despite this, cases of Legionnaires' disease are documented annually. The CDC estimates that 10,000 to 15,000 people are infected with the disease each year in the United States alone. Although *Legionella pneu-*

American Nobel Prize Winners in Physiology or Medicine

Year	Scientist
1970	Julius Axelrod
1971	Earl W. Sutherland Jr.
1972	Gerald M. Edelman
1973	No award given to an American
1974	George E. Palade
1975	David Baltimore
	Renato Dulbecco
	Howard M. Temin
1976	Baruch S. Blumberg
	D. Carleton Gajdusek
1977	Roger Guillemin
	Andrew V. Schalley
	Rosalyn S. Yalow
1978	Daniel Nathans
	Hamilton O. Smith
1979	Allan M. Cormack

mophilia favors warm, still water, it can be found in cooling towers and wells. It can also be found in trace amounts in lakes and rivers. Antibiotics are effective in treating the disease, which is not contagious.

THE SWINE FLU SCARE

While Legionnaires' disease was making headlines across the country in 1976, another possible epidemic had been panicking Americans for months. In February of that year, an outbreak of respiratory disease occurred among army recruits at Fort Dix, New Jersey, resulting in the death of one recruit. The Centers for Disease Control (CDC), the federal government agency responsible for developing and applying disease prevention and control, examined the recruit's body, finding an influenza virus similar to the swine flu virus. An investigation of the other recruits found thirteen similar cases. Concern began to spread.

Lyme Disease

In the summer of 1975, residents around Lyme, Connecticut, started to develop a strange combination of shared symptoms: rashes, headaches, and pain and stiffness in their joints similar to arthritis. At first, doctors were baffled not only by the symptoms but also by the fact that many of those affected were children. Arthritis in children (called juvenile arthritis) is rare and is not contagious. Medical researchers investigating the mysterious outbreak were soon convinced they were looking at a new disease.

Piecing together the facts of the case, researchers discovered that all the victims lived near wooded areas and first noticed their symptoms in summer or fall. Many victims reported an unusual bull's-eye-shaped rash that appeared weeks before their symptoms arose. Researchers connected this rash to a similar one thought to be caused by a tick bite that had been reported in parts of Europe since the beginning of the twentieth century. Warm wooded areas are a perfect breeding ground for ticks, so researchers began collecting and examining ticks from the wooded areas around Lyme.

In 1977, researchers named the disease after the town around which the initial victims lived. A few years later, they discovered that the disease is caused by a spiral-shaped bacterium called *Borrelia burgdorferi.* It is carried and spread by ticks that infect deer, mice, and domestic animals, as well as humans. Antibiotics are the only weapons against the disease, which spread throughout the country. Annually, about sixteen thousand infections occur in the United States.

In 1918, the swine flu virus had been the cause of a pandemic that killed twenty million people worldwide, including six hundred thousand in the United States. Since the late 1920s, the virus could be found only in pigs. This meant that in the 1970s, no human being under the age of fifty could have built up antibodies against the virus. (Antibodies are substances produced by the body to provide immunity or protection against a specific foreign substance.)

Believing that a new highly contagious strain of swine flu virus posed a threat to humans, the CDC recommended a major effort to produce a vaccine against it. In response, President Gerald R. Ford (1913–) announced in March 1976 an unprecedented nationwide campaign to vac-

Tuskegee Syphilis Study

In 1972, a breaking news story shocked the nation. For forty years, from 1932 to 1972, 399 African American men from Macon County, Alabama, were denied treatment for syphilis, a highly contagious sexually transmitted disease. The men, almost all of them poor and undereducated, were part of an experiment conducted at the medical facilities of Tuskegee Institute by physicians of the U.S. Public Health Service. The aim of the experiment was to document the long-term effects of the disease on the human body.

Told they were being treated for "bad blood," the men were given only aspirin, free medical exams, free meals, and burial insurance. Even though penicillin, a cure for syphilis, had become available in 1943, the men were deliberately denied such proper treatment.

By the time the experiment was exposed and halted, twenty-eight of the men had died directly of syphilis. One hundred more had died of related complications from the disease. Many of the men's wives had contracted syphilis from their husbands. In turn, many of these women had given birth to children with congenital syphilis (the disease was present in their bodies when they were born). The National Association for the Advancement of Colored People (NAACP) filed suit against the U.S. government on behalf of the participants in the experiment. In addition to a $9 million settlement, the government agreed to provide free medical and burial services to all living participants. It also extended treatment to the wives, widows, and children who had been infected because of the experiment. Shortly afterward, the U.S. Congress passed legislation aimed at preventing a recurrence of such callous governmental research practices. On May 16, 1997, President Bill Clinton apologized on behalf of the nation to the men and their families.

cinate all 210 million Americans against swine flu. The U.S. Congress budgeted $135 million to finance the effort. After a variety of delays and concerns about proper dosages, the vaccination program finally began on October 1. More than one million Americans were vaccinated during the first ten days of the program.

Then things went wrong. Reports of deaths following vaccinations surfaced first in Pittsburgh, Pennsylvania, then elsewhere around the country. Three weeks after the program started, forty-one people had died of side effects from the vaccine. A few weeks later, some people reported symptoms of nervous system disorders following vaccinations. Finally, on December 16, the federal government suspended the mass-vaccination program. By that time, forty-five million people had received the vaccine. Fifty-two had died of side effects and over five hundred had been hospitalized for disorders and impairments. At that time, not one new case of swine flu had been reported in the United States since the Fort Dix incident.

In early 1977, the federal government commissioned a review of what had become known as the "swine flu fiasco." Although it was clear that a mass epidemic is always cause for concern, the government realized it should have waited for evidence of a significant spread of the virus before proceeding with a nationwide vaccination program. Instead, it had acted too quickly to prevent an epidemic that never occurred.

For More Information

BOOKS

Berger, Melvin. *Disease Detectives.* New York: Crowell, 1978.

Fixx, James F. *The Complete Book of Running.* New York: Random House, 1977.

Jones, James H. *Bad Blood: The Tuskegee Syphilis Experiment.* Revised ed. New York: Free Press, 1992.

Quinlan, Joseph, and Julia Quinlan, with Phyllis Battelle. *Karen Ann: The Quinlans Tell Their Story.* Garden City, NY: Doubleday, 1977.

Straus, Eugene. *Rosalyn Yalow, Nobel Laureate: Her Life and Work in Medicine.* New York: Plenum Press, 1998.

WEB SITES

A History of HMOs. [Online] http://www.hapcorp.org/main/history_hmo.htm (accessed on February 27, 2002).

The Influenza A/New Jersey (Swine Flu) Vaccine and Guillain-Barré Syndrome: The Arguments for a Causal Association. [Online] http://www.hsph.harvard.edu/Organizations/DDIL/swineflu.html (accessed on February 27, 2002).

Karen Ann Quinlan: 1954–1985. [Online] http://www.karenannquinlanhospice.org/new_page_3.htm (accessed on February 27, 2002).

Legionellosis: Legionnaire's Disease (LD) and Pontiac Fever. [Online] http://www.cdc.gov/ncidod/dbmd/diseaseinfo/legionellosis_g.htm (accessed on February 27, 2002).

chapter seven

Science and Technology

1970: The floppy disk is introduced for storing computer information.

1970: **January 21** The Boeing 747, the first jumbo jet, is put into commercial service.

1970: **April 11** The *Apollo 13* mission begins. Two days, later an oxygen leak and fire disable the spacecraft, and the astronauts barely make it home safely.

1970: **April 22** The first Earth Day is celebrated.

1971: Intel introduces the first silicon computer chip (microprocessor).

1971: Texas Instruments introduces the first pocket calculator, weighing 2.5 pounds and costing around $150.

1971: **May 8** Mars probe *Mariner 8* is launched. It suffers engine failure, falls back to Earth, and lands north of Puerto Rico.

1972: The California State Board of Education demands that textbooks give equal weight to creationism as a type of evolutionary theory.

1972: The large particle accelerator at Fermi National Accelerator Laboratory in Batavia, Illinois, begins operation.

1972: **March 22** The *Pioneer 10* space probe is launched to explore the outer planets; on June 13, 1983, it becomes the first human-created object to leave the solar system.

1972: **June 14** Following warnings that DDT is interfering with the reproduction of birds and is potentially toxic to humans, the Environmental Protection Agency announces a ban on most uses of pesticides, beginning December 31.

1972: **December 7** *Apollo 17*, the last manned lunar landing, is launched.

1973: The push-through tab is introduced in soft drinks and beer cans.

1973: Scientists first express concern to the public that genetic engineering might produce new and dangerous microorganisms.

1973: **April 5** *Pioneer 11* is launched. In 1979 it becomes the first human-made object to fly by Saturn.

1973: **May 25** The first Skylab mission is launched. A three-man crew conducts experiments for twenty-eight days in this orbiting space station.

1974: Scientists warm that chlorofluorocarbons (CFCs) used as propellants in spray cans may be destroying the ozone layer of Earth's atmosphere.

1974: Hewlett Packard introduces a programmable pocket calculator.

1974: November 24 A three-million-year-old humanlike skeleton is found in Ethiopia and is named Lucy.

1975: The first personal computer, the Altair 8800, is introduced in kit form.

1975: July 15 The American-Soviet *Apollo-Soyuz* orbiting space station is launched.

1975: August 20 *Viking 1* is launched. It begins sending pictures from Mars in June 1976.

1976: The French-English supersonic jet Concorde begins regular passenger service.

1976: Genentech, the first company devoted to creating products through genetic engineering, is founded near San Francisco, California.

1976: September 13 The U.S. Naval Academy of Sciences says that CFCs, especially those in aerosol cans, endanger the ozone layer.

1977: Deep-sea "chimneys" are found near the Galapagos Islands, where warm water allows bacteria, giant clams, and tube worms to survive beyond the reach of sunlight.

1977: The Apple II, the first successful personal computer, is introduced.

1977: August 20 and September 5 Space probes *Voyager 1* and *Voyager 2* are launched on a journey to Jupiter and the outer planets.

1978: Lois Gibbs of the Love Canal Homeowners' Association demonstrates that residents' health is being adversely affected by a nearby toxic-waste dump.

1978: Apple releases the first disk drive for use with personal computers.

1978: March 15 CFCs are banned as spray propellants.

1978: May 20 and August 8 Two Pioneer space probes are launched toward Venus.

1979: VisiCalc introduces a spreadsheet program for personal computers, allowing users who know nothing about programming to use a business application for computers for the first time.

1979: Evidence dating from about sixty-five million years ago in deep-sea cores shows that there are no fossils for a period of about one hundred thousand years.

1979: March 28 Partial accidental meltdown begins in the reactor at Unit 2 of Three Mile Island nuclear power plant in Harrisburg, Pennsylvania.

1979: July 11 Skylab falls into the atmosphere, breaking up over Australia and the Indian Ocean.

Overview

American attitudes toward science and technology in the 1970s evolved from a complete faith in its ability to promote progress and prosperity to a more cautious view of its benefits. At the beginning of the decade, scientific advances opened up a whole new world. Humans landed on the Moon with such regularity that the public eventually paid little attention, considering these extraordinary events commonplace. After missions to the Moon, the space program expanded its exploration of space, sending out probes to other planets and placing a space station in orbit around Earth.

While some scientists kept their eyes on the sky, others focused downward, scanning the ground for human fossils and clues to human beginnings. The search for the origin of life on the planet even extended to the seas as scientists and explorers probed the deep reaches of the oceans, discovering mysterious and wonderful creatures never seen before. Television brought images of those discoveries into the living rooms of ordinary Americans.

Televised views of Earth, both from underwater and from space, raised awareness of the fragility of the planet during the 1970s. Science not only sent humans to the Moon but was also responsible for developing chemicals that poisoned the crops, forests, and swamps in Vietnam. Toxic waste and pesticides in American soil and water, by-products of scientific and industrial progress, caused great concern to Americans. Rallies and demonstrations to stop the spread of poisons arose in communities small and large across the country. Pressure on the government resulted in federal bans on chemicals that had been part of everyday life.

By the end of the decade, many Americans saw science's ability to harm the planet as well as its capacity to benefit humanity. Nuclear meltdowns, toxic waste dumps, and space stations falling from the sky dominated the news. Technological and scientific advances continued, but Americans welcomed them with caution.

Robert Ballard (1942–) Geologist and ocean explorer Robert Ballard, along with his colleagues, discovered a thriving community of crabs, eels, and tube worms on the ocean floor near the Galapagos Islands in 1977. These animals existed far below the reach of sunlight, at the mouths of volcano-like structures, areas previously thought to be too hot and remote to support life. Ballard and his team theorized that these deep ocean vents spewed sulfur-rich water, which fed bacteria living nearby; larger animals in turn fed on the bacteria. This process, the scientists suggested, might be similar to how life on Earth began. *Photo reproduced by permission of AP/Wide World Photos.*

Jacques Cousteau (1910–1997) In the 1970s, French oceanographer and explorer Jacques Cousteau exposed millions of American viewers (and others around the world) to life under the sea through the ABC television documentary series *The Undersea World of Jacques Cousteau.* Aboard his ship, the *Calypso,* Cousteau, his sons, and his crew explored marine life and environments around the world, raising awareness of environmental dangers threatening Earth's oceans. In 1970, he also produced twelve one-hour episodes of a series titled *The Undersea Odyssey of the "Calypso,"* followed by six more shows in 1973. *Photo reproduced by permission of the Granger Collection.*

Arno Penzias (1933–) Astrophysicist Arno Penzias and his colleague Robert W. Wilson (1936–) shared the 1978 Nobel Prize for physics for a discovery they had made in 1965. While scanning an area of space where no radio waves were expected, they detected a weak hiss of radio noise. Further exploration found this unexpected noise coming from all areas of space. Applying another astronomer's theory, Penzias and Wilson determined the mysterious radio signal was radiation (now called the cosmic microwave background) left over from the formation of the universe. This discovery substantiated the big bang theory of the creation of the universe. *Photo reproduced by permission of the Corbis Corporation.*

Edward O. Wilson (1929–) Biologist Edward O. Wilson combined biology and culture when he asserted in his 1975 book *Sociobiology* that many social behaviors, such as aggression and altruism, were not learned but were built into a person's genes. Critics argued that Wilson's approach allowed undesirable human behaviors (rape, for instance) to be viewed as natural. In 1978, Wilson published *On Human Nature,* in which he clarified his controversial views and discussed free will, ethics, and human development. The book won the 1979 Pulitzer Prize for general nonfiction. *Photo reproduced by permission of AP/Wide World Photos.*

SPACE: FINAL MOON MISSIONS, THE FIRST SPACE STATION, AND DISASTERS

Perhaps the best symbol of American faith in science during the 1970s was the excitement surrounding the exploration of space. Millions of Americans (and millions more around the world) had watched the first Moon walks on television in 1969 with amazement. Within just a few years, however, what once had amazed began to seem routine. The space program, especially the Moon landings early in the decade, seemed to symbolize the strength of the United States and its unlimited technical and scientific capabilities. Regular and precise, the program quickly eased its way into American culture. Products first developed for the astronauts soon became available to the general public. Tang, a popular orange-flavored drink, was originally "the breakfast of astronauts." Food Sticks, a sweet, chewy snack, and Actifed, a nasal decongestant, were advertised as having been taken on Apollo flights.

In 1971 and 1972, there were two moon or lunar landings a year, each nearly identical to the others. The landings combined both public relations and hard science. Launched in early 1971, the *Apollo 14* mission (Apollo was the lunar-landing program) included astronaut Alan Shepard hitting a golf ball on the Moon. On the next Apollo mission, astronaut David Scott demonstrated the effects of zero atmosphere by dropping a hammer and a feather at the same time. Astronaut James Irwin kept the camera rolling as both struck the Moon's surface at the same time. Though lighthearted, these "experiments" confirmed scientific theories. On a more serious note, each lunar mission brought back bigger bags of Moon rocks, which enabled scientists to learn more about the composition of the Moon. The metallic composition of the lunar surface turned out to be significantly different from Earth's, encouraging fresh speculation about the origins of the two bodies.

The driving force behind the passion for space exploration was the cold war, a period of political tension between the former Soviet Union and the United States. Ever since the Soviet unmanned satellite *Sputnik I* had beaten the Americans into space in 1957, the "space race " had been on. Each side was concerned about the potential military advantage the other might gain through superiority in space. Early in the 1970s, it appeared the American advantage was in Moon landings, while the Soviets excelled in extended stays in space.

To counter that supposed Soviet superiority, the National Aeronautics and Space Administration (NASA) launched the first U.S. space station,

Creation of the Silicon Chip

The computers of the early 1960s were mammoth machines, requiring entire rooms to house them. They were also so expensive that only large organizations and the government could afford them. Later, minicomputers were produced, which were more attractive to businesses and researchers in size and cost. The breakthrough that made the personal microcomputer possible came in 1971, when Theodore Hoff of Intel squeezed 2,300 transistors onto a thin chip of silicon, creating the microprocessor chip. This history-changing achievement converted much of the power of the bulky mainframe into a small chip that could be held in the palm of the hand.

Skylab, in May 1973. The station was designed for astronomical observation and studies on the effects of weightlessness. NASA scientists also hoped the station could provide a permanent human presence in space. During its six years of operation, a total of nine astronauts on three separate missions spent twenty-eight, fifty-nine, and eighty-four days aboard Skylab, setting new space endurance records.

The cold war thawed briefly in the summer of 1975 when Apollo and Soyuz (the Soviet equivalent of the Apollo program) modules met and docked in space. Many thought the docking of the two nations' spacecrafts would soon lead to future international space stations, but that would not occur for another two decades. After two days of joint scientific experiments, the two spacecraft parted and returned to Earth, concluding the final Apollo mission.

The excitement surrounding the space program that marked the beginning of the 1970s soon faded as Americans confronted more pressing social issues: health, education, poverty, crime, and drug control. Disasters also struck the space program. In 1967, three astronauts had died on the launch pad when fire swept through the cabin of the *Apollo 1* spacecraft. Three years later, three astronauts on the way to the Moon in *Apollo 13* were almost stranded in space when the oxygen tanks on the spacecraft blew up and emptied. Using the lunar module as a lifeboat, the astronauts headed back to Earth. To conserve oxygen and electricity, they lowered the temperature inside the module to 38°F. Even so, the astronauts barely made it back to Earth before their limited oxygen supply was depleted.

OPPOSITE PAGE A view of Earth from space. A driving force behind the passion for early space exploration was the cold war between the United States and the Soviet Union. ***Courtesy of the U.S. National Aeronautics and Space Administration.***

These accidents (and mishaps suffered by the Soviet space program) raised public concern about the progress of space flight. When Skylab fell from the sky in 1979, that concern turned to scorn. In June of that year, NASA announced the $2.6 billion space station was in a decaying orbit

and the equipment designed to boost it higher had failed. To make matters worse, Skylab did not fall into one of the world's oceans, as NASA had hoped. Instead, it landed in western Australia. Luckily, the area was sparsely populated and no one was injured.

By the end of the decade, NASA's image was tarnished. Man never set foot on the Moon again after 1972 (and would not for the rest of the century). Beyond space probes (unmanned spacecraft) sent out to explore other planets and the outer reaches of our solar system, it seemed in the late 1970s that the era of space flight had ended.

LUCY AND THE SEARCH FOR EARLY HUMANS

While some scientists in the 1970s probed space to answer questions about creation, others looked underground on Earth, including Kenyan paleoanthropologist Richard Leakey (1944–) and his father, English archaeologist and anthropologist Louis Leakey (1903–1972). *National Geographic* television specials made the Leakeys famous by celebrating their discoveries of the fossils of ancestral humans, large-brained tool users in East Africa.

When the $2.6 billion Skylab fell from the sky in 1979 it helped tarnish the reputation of the U.S. space program. **Courtesy of the U.S. National Aeronautics and Space Administration.**

The First Jumbo Jet

A revolution in air travel occurred on January 21, 1970, with the first commercial flight of the Boeing 747. Previously, the largest commercial plane was the Boeing 707, which could carry 132 people. In comparison, the 747 could accommodate up to 490 passengers—almost four times as many. The press labeled the jet an "air bus." Despite its size, its titanium body made it light enough to fly great distances. The 747 had a tremendous range, capable of going forty-six hundred nautical miles without refueling. These two features made it an ideal plane for transcontinental flights. By the end of the 1970s, millions of people had traveled in 747s.

Initially, experts did not believe the 747 would be a success. No airport in the world at the time had terminals that could accommodate its wide body. It was also believed that the future of air travel lay in supersonics, planes that can travel faster than the speed of sound. But supersonics produce a sonic boom as they take off, and the idea that this noise could become an everyday occurrence soon swayed public opinion against supersonics.

In 1974, a discovery near Hadar in the Afar region in Ethiopia shifted attention away from the Leakeys to American anthropologist Donald Johanson (1943–). While surveying the rugged landscape in the Afar region, Johanson and a team of anthropologists found the skeletal remains of a three-million-year-old hominid (member of the family of primates that includes modern humans). The fossil was older and more complete than any hominid ever found before. The shape of the pelvis showed it to be female, while the knee joint and thigh revealed that she walked upright. Her brain size was about one-third that of modern humans, yet larger than any apelike ancestor to have come before. In life, she would have stood about 3.5 feet tall, with long arms, a V-shaped jaw, and a large protruding face. Whimsically, members of the team named her Lucy, after the Beatles' song "Lucy in the Sky with Diamonds," which had been playing over and over during the celebration at the team's camp the night of the discovery. Her Swahili name was more respectful: *Denkanesh,* meaning "you are wonderful."

Debates between anthropologists quickly ensued after Johanson's discovery. Initially, Johanson argued that Lucy's upright stature and humanlike features made her a member of the genus *Homo*. This would

American Nobel Prize Winners in Chemistry or Physics

Year	Scientist(s)	Field
1970	No award given to an American	
1971	No award given to an American	
1972	Christian Boehmer Anfinsen	Chemistry
	Stanford Moore	
	William H. Stein	
	John Bardeen	Physics
	Leon N. Cooper	
	John R. Schrieffer	
1973	Ivar Glaevar	Physics
1974	Paul J. Flory	Chemistry
1975	L. James Rainwater	Physics
1976	Burton Richter	Physics
	Samuel C. C. Ting	
1977	Philip Warren Anderson	Physics
	John Hasbrouck van Vleck	
1978	Arno Penzias	Physics
	Robert Wilson	
1979	Herbert C. Brown	Chemistry
	Steven Weinberg	Physics
	Sheldon Glashow	

place her in the same classification as modern humans and the Leakeys' more modern fossils. After considerable discussion, anthropologists decided to assign Lucy to the genus *Australopithecus*. The assignment meant that both Richard Leakey and Johanson could now claim they had found the remains of the earliest human. Leakey believed, however, that *Australopithecus* was part of a branch of the evolutionary tree that had eventually died out, while Johanson thought Lucy was an ancestor of modern humans.

Further discoveries merely intensified the disagreement between the two men. In 1975, Johanson's team found a large group of 3.7-million-year-old hominid fossils together, representing at least thirteen individuals, including an infant and several juveniles. These fossils became known as the "first family." Taken together, along with a skull found in Tanzania by Mary Leakey, Richard's mother, Johanson and his collaborators argued that they had found a new species. They called it *Australopithecus afarensis*, meaning the southern ape of the Afar region.

SPACESHIP EARTH: THE RISE OF ENVIRONMENTALISM

As interest in human evolution increased sharply in the 1970s, so did a corresponding interest in the fate of the planet. The decade launched unprecedented activism in support of the environment. Not since the years immediately following 1910 had ecology seemed so important to so many people—students, scientists, politicians, businesspeople, and most ordinary citizens. Terms such as Earth Day, environmental ethics, and the Gaia hypothesis arose during the 1970s to become part of the common American vocabulary.

Earth Day was first celebrated throughout America on April 22, 1970. On that day (and every April 22 since), millions of Americans participated in demonstrations, teach-ins, and community cleanup projects for the environment. The observance, coordinated by a group of organizers in Washington, D.C., was modeled after the anti-Vietnam War demonstrations of 1969. It was intended to galvanize public sentiment in support of environmental issues.

American anthropologist Donald Johanson displaying the skull of the three-million-year-old hominid Lucy. **Reproduced by permission of the Corbis Corporation.**

People around the country celebrated in a variety of ways. In New York, tens of thousands marched down Fifth Avenue. In Boston, a small group was arrested at Logan Airport protesting noise pollution and the development of supersonic jets. Students in Minneapolis and Chicago gained entrance to stockholders' meetings of major polluters, including General Electric and Commonwealth Edison, to demand changes in policy and priorities.

That first Earth Day launched the beginning of an environmental awareness in the United States and later around the world. It made people realize that some sense of environmental ethics, or responsibility, should

The First Uses of Fiber Optics

Optical fiber is a thin strand of glass or plastic capable of transmitting light from one point to another. The thin, extremely pure glass of an optical fiber, surrounded by a reflective casing, can bend light. This makes it possible to use light, specifically light generated by lasers, in place of electricity. Light can be carried faster, more cheaply, and more efficiently than electrical signals, which can be affected by motors, electrical generators, power lines, or lightning storms. Sounds are converted into a pattern of light, transmitted, received at the other end, then converted back into sound.

By the beginning of the 1970s, researchers believed that fiber optics had tremendous potential to improve the clarity and speed of telephone signals: A single hair-thin optical fiber could carry as many messages as a thick copper-wire cable containing 512 wires. One of the first such uses of fiber optics was in 1977 in Chicago. Two offices of Bell Telephone and a third for customers were successfully connected by light-carrying glass fibers. In 1978, the telephones at Disney World were linked through fiber optics; Disney also used them for video transmission, lighting, and alarm systems.

be developed and applied to their daily lives. Unfortunately, not everyone shared this belief. Interior Secretary Walter Hickel, used the occasion of the first Earth Day to announce the approval of the proposed Alaskan oil pipeline. Environmental groups had opposed the pipeline in the belief that it would destroy the unique habitat of the tundra and disturb migratory patterns of many animals.

Despite such moves on the part of certain businesses and the government, an environmental consciousness arose in many people. Once they became aware that they had some sort of responsibility toward the natural world, they began to act. Numerous skirmishes between citizens and industry soon developed over the presence of artificially produced chemicals in food and the environment. Toxic-waste sites, the pesticide DDT, and chlorofluorocarbons (CFCs) became rallying causes for those who believed the environment needed protection from big business. In 1972, the U.S. Environmental Protection Agency (newly formed in 1970) disregarded the objections of pesticide companies and banned DDT as dangerous to humans and wildlife. Many people found in this action a symbol of the need for strong oversight of science and industry.

At the beginning of the 1970s, CFCs could be found in nearly every household, not only as aerosol propellants in products such as hairsprays and deodorants, but also in foam mattresses, air conditioners, and refrigerators. In 1973, some scientists argued that accumulation of CFCs could erode the protective ozone layer of the upper atmosphere. The "ozone hole" would expose Earth to increasing amounts of ultraviolet radiation from the Sun, resulting in higher human skin cancer rates, lower crop yields, and a cooler global climate. Following these warnings, chemical companies, notably DuPont, insisted that if CFCs were dangerous, they would stop production immediately to protect the environment. They then did nothing for five years and lobbied Congress to postpone efforts to restrict the chemicals, calling for more studies. In 1978, the U.S. Food and Drug Administration (FDA) stepped in, banning CFCs in aerosol products in the United States.

The public's view of the environment and of Earth itself changed drastically over the course of the decade. Many had come to view the planet as a living superorganism that can regulate its own environment, maintaining conditions that are favorable for life to survive on it. It is the living things on Earth that give the planet this ability. This idea, called the Gaia (pronounced GAY-ah) hypothesis, was proposed by English chemist James Lovelock (1919–) in 1979. Although the idea is still scientifically controversial, it places great emphasis on the quality of Earth's environment and the role humans play in Earth's destiny.

TOXIC AND NUCLEAR DISASTERS: LOVE CANAL AND THREE MILE ISLAND

Two high-profile industrial disasters in the late 1970s dramatically confirmed what many Americans had come to believe: The environment and human health were intertwined and must be protected accordingly.

In the 1930s and 1940s, corporations and citizens did not worry too much about what happened to the chemicals left over from industrial processes. While regulations existed, enforcement was haphazard or nonexistent. Corporations such as Hooker Company in Niagara Falls, New York, which made pesticides, plastics, and other chemicals, mostly just sealed them in fifty-five-gallon metal drums and left them someplace nearby. For Hooker, one convenient place was Love Canal, part of a Great Lakes canal system begun in the late nineteenth century but never completed. While children played and swam nearby, Hooker dumped more than twenty-one thousand tons of chemicals into Love Canal, then filled it in with dirt. In 1953, the company gave the covered-over lot to the town for an elementary school and a playground.

As young families built homes near the elementary school, many noticed that their basements leaked. Some thought they noticed chemical smells and strange colors in water that leaked in. Few knew much about the history of chemical dumping. A dramatic sign that something was amiss came in 1974, when one family's backyard pool rose two feet out of the ground. When they removed it, blue, yellow, and purple chemicals suddenly rushed in where the pool had been. By 1977, after several years of unusually heavy rain and snowfall, the former canal was turning into a marsh, and chemicals were noticeably seeping into surrounding soil and streams.

Families wanted to move from the area, but were stranded as their homes had become worthless. In 1978, after repeated requests, state, local, and federal officials finally tested the air and water in Love Canal basements. The results proved that the health of the residents in the area was in danger. The studies had found conclusive evidence of an abnormally

The serious incident at the Three Mile Island nuclear plant left Americans cautious about the safety of the nuclear power industry. **Reproduced by permission of AP/Wide World Photos.**

The Lasting Effects of Agent Orange

During the Vietnam War (1954–75), the U.S. military used several herbicidal (plant-killing) preparations to destroy forests and crops in South Vietnam, thereby depriving the enemy of hiding places and food. One of these preparations, a combination of two herbicides commonly used to kill weeds, was known as Agent Orange. Named for the orange identification stripe painted on the fifty-five-gallon barrels in which it was transported, Agent Orange was developed by the army in the 1950s as an alternative to biological weapons.

Agent Orange was sprayed over the landscape from cargo planes, boats, trucks, and backpacks. In 1971, following criticism from the National Academy of Sciences, international organizations, and the American public, the military agreed to stop using Agent Orange. By that time, approximately nineteen million gallons of the herbicide had been sprayed, destroying almost all plant life covering over four million acres.

The damage to plant life and animal habitats in South Vietnam caused by Agent Orange is still visible. The most severe damage occurred in mangrove forests along coastal areas. Scientists estimate that full recovery of these forests to their native state will take at least one hundred years.

More serious are the possible long-term health effects on the U.S. soldiers and others exposed to Agent Orange. Many Vietnam veterans suffered health problems when they returned home, but government officials said Agent Orange did not cause the soldiers' symptoms. At issue in these claims is dioxin, a by-product of Agent Orange. Medical researchers believe dioxin, an extremely toxic chemical, can cause birth defects, cancer, and nerve damage. While dioxin was present in all samples of Agent Orange tested, federal chemists and health officials thought it existed in quantities too small to be harmful. Despite lawsuits, the U.S. Department of Defense never agreed that Agent Orange was responsible for damaging the health of veterans.

high rate of miscarriages and birth defects. The announcement left homeowners angry, frightened, and frustrated. They organized the Love Canal Homeowners' Association to pressure officials to buy their homes so they, in turn, could buy homes elsewhere and move.

Creation of the Compact Disc

Thomas Edison's invention of the phonograph, or record player, in 1877 allowed recorded sound to be reproduced for the first time. Sound produced by a phonograph is first recorded as a spiral groove with varying amounts of indentation on a disk known as a record. A needle, or stylus, attached to a tone arm rides in the groove, vibrating as it travels over the uneven surface. Those vibrations are transferred through the tone arm to other elements in the phonograph that convert the vibrations into sound waves. Eventually, however, the groove and needle wear out, and the sound quality of a record deteriorates.

In 1972, less than one hundred years after Edison's invention, optoelectronics (branch of electronics dealing with light) made the development of the compact disc, or CD, practical. Lasers could burn small holes, or pits, into a microscopic layer on the surface of a disc. Other lasers could detect the pits and smooth areas on the disc, converting that information first into electrical impulses, then into sound waves. CD recordings came out stunningly clear, held more information than phonograph records, and suffered almost no wear. The first commercially successful audio or music CDs were introduced in Japan and Europe in 1982 and in the United States the following year.

Shortly after the formation of the association, President Jimmy Carter (1924–) proclaimed the area a federal disaster area, freeing up funds for residents of the south end of the canal to relocate. However, this still left those in surrounding areas unable to move, despite growing evidence of high rates of cancer, kidney and bladder troubles, birth defects, miscarriages, nervous disorders, and other illnesses. After six months, the state agreed to pay for pregnant women and those with small children to be relocated, yet it forced them to return to Love Canal when the children grew older. Unsatisfied, residents continued to sign petitions, write letters, and hold demonstrations.

Then in 1980, the state confirmed what some had long suspected: Among the chemicals at Love Canal was dioxin, a highly toxic substance. When this news was released, the state finally agreed to buy the nearby homes. After two years of anxiety and activism, homeowners there finally could afford to move. A decade later, the government put these houses on the market again, and a new community of homeowners moved in amid controversy over whether the site was still contaminated with toxic waste.

While residents around Love Canal faced the threat of toxic chemicals, those living in the shadow of the Three Mile Island nuclear power plant near Harrisburg, Pennsylvania, faced the threat of radiation. In the 1970s, as people in the United States used increasing amounts of electric energy, nuclear power promised to be cheaper and cleaner than the burning of fossil fuels, which created air pollution. When an oil embargo by countries in the Middle East in 1973–74 created shortages and high gas prices, atomic energy seemed to offer a way for the nation to achieve energy independence. Support for nuclear power ran high.

But events on March 28, 1979, would quickly erode that support. At 4:00 A.M. a mechanical failure of the cooling system of the Three Mile Island plant was compounded by operator error. Technicians in the control room of the Unit 2 reactor, misunderstanding the nature of the problem, shut off all water to the reactor. With no water cooling it, the reactor became extremely hot—in excess of five thousand degrees—and began to melt. Within hours there was enough radiation in the containment dome to kill a person in minutes, and some radiation began leaking into the environment. It was another two days before the public learned how serious the accident was and officials began talking about a meltdown. Pregnant women and small children were evacuated from the area. Ironically, the worst danger of a meltdown passed before the evacuation order was given; by then, the reactor was underwater again. Nine days later, believing the core had cooled sufficiently enough, public officials encouraged nearby residents to return to their homes. Yet a year later, the reactor was still hot.

There were no apparent injuries at Three Mile Island, but the incident dealt the nuclear power industry a blow that sent it into sharp decline. In April 1979, a Gallup poll found that 66 percent of Americans believed nuclear power to be unsafe. Although that number declined to 50 percent nine months later, the event created an enduring caution in the country about the nuclear power industry.

For More Information

BOOKS

Collins, Michael. *Liftoff: The Story of America's Adventure in Space.* New York: Grove, 1988.

Hampton, Wilborn. *Meltdown : A Race Against Nuclear Disaster at Three Mile Island.* Cambridge, MA: Candlewick Press, 2001.

Johanson, Donald C. and James Shreeve. *Lucy's Child: The Discovery of a Human Ancestor.* New York: Morrow, 1989.

Kennedy, Gregory P. *Apollo to the Moon.* New York: Chelsea House, 1992.

Stefoff, Rebecca. *The American Environmental Movement.* New York: Facts on File, 1995.

Wilson, Edward O. *On Human Nature.* Cambridge, MA: Harvard University Press, 1988.

Wilson, Edward O. *Sociobiology: The New Synthesis.* Cambridge, MA: Harvard University Press, 2000.

WEB SITES

Love Canal Documents. [Online] http://www.epa.gov/history/topics/lovecanal/ (accessed on February 27, 2002).

Meltdown at Three Mile Island. [Online] http://www.pbs.org/wgbh/amex/three/ (accessed on February 27, 2002).

Skylab. [Online] http://www-pao.ksc.nasa.gov/kscpao/history/skylab/skylab.htm (accessed on February 27, 2002).

chapter eight **Sports**

1970: January 26 NFL commissioner Pete Rozelle announces a four-year, $142-million contract with the three major television networks to broadcast professional football games.

1970: August 12 In a case brought by Philadelphia Phillies outfielder Curt Flood, federal court judge Ben Cooper rules that a 1922 U.S. Supreme Court decision finding that organized baseball does not violate antitrust laws is still binding. The Major League Baseball Players' Association announces it will take the case to the U.S. Supreme Court.

1970: October 26 Muhammad Ali knocks out Jerry Quarry in three rounds in his first fight since his license to box was revoked in 1967.

1971: February 28 Jack Nicklaus becomes the first golfer to win the PGA championship twice.

1971: April 27 Professional baseball player Curt Flood, who tested baseball's reserve clause, announces his retirement.

1971: May 7 The American Basketball Association (ABA) and the National Basketball Association (NBA) seek congressional approval to merge.

1972: February 3 to 13 The Winter Olympics are held in Sapporo, Japan.

1972: June 19 The U.S. Supreme Court reaffirms the exemption of professional baseball from antitrust laws.

1972: August 22 to September 10 The Summer Olympics are held in Munich, West Germany.

1972: September 4 Swimmer Mark Spitz wins his seventh gold medal in the Summer Olympic Games.

1972: September 5 Arab terrorists kill two Israeli athletes and kidnap nine others at the Summer Olympics. The games are suspended for two days after the terrorist attack.

1973: January 14 The Miami Dolphins win the Super Bowl, becoming the first professional football team to complete a season undefeated.

1973: February 25 Baseball owners and players sign a three-year contract agreeing to submit salary disputes to binding arbitration.

1973: September 21 Billie Jean King defeats Bobby Riggs in a highly publicized tennis match billed as the "Battle of the Sexes."

1974: April 8 Hank Aaron of the Atlanta Braves breaks Babe Ruth's career home run record, hitting number 715.

1974: October 3 Frank Robinson is named manager of the Cleveland Indians, becoming the first African American manager in major-league baseball.

1974: **October 30** Muhammad Ali knocks out George Foreman in the eighth round to regain the heavyweight boxing championship.

1975: **February 16** Jimmy Connors becomes the first player to win three straight national indoor tennis tournaments.

1975: **July 5** Arthur Ashe defeats Jimmy Connors to win the Wimbledon men's singles championship, becoming the first African American to do so.

1975: **December 30** A federal court judge rules that free-agency in the NFL violates antitrust laws.

1976: **February 4 to 15** The Winter Olympics are held in Innsbruck, Austria.

1976: **June 17** The NBA accepts four of the six teams in the ABA in a merger recommended by a federal judge to settle antitrust litigation.

1976: **July 17 to August 1** The Summer Olympics are held in Montreal, Canada.

1976: **August 27** Renee Richards, a transsexual, is barred from competition in the U.S. Open tennis tournament.

1977: **June 11** Seattle Slew wins horse racing's Triple Crown. He is the tenth Triple Crown winner in history and the first undefeated winner.

1977: **September 10** Chris Evert wins her third straight U.S. Open women's tennis championship.

1977: **October 26** The NFL signs an agreement with the three major networks for rights to televise NFL games in exchange for $576 million to $656 million.

1978: **June 18** First-year professional golfer Nancy Lopez breaks the LPGA record for consecutive wins, accumulating record earnings for a rookie of $153,336.

1978: **July 15** Jack Nicklaus wins his third British Open golf tournament.

1978: **December 5** Pete Rose, a free agent in the professional baseball draft, signs a $3.2-million contract with the Philadelphia Phillies, making him baseball's highest-paid player.

1979: **January 21** The Pittsburgh Steelers win their third Super Bowl, the first NFL team to do so.

1979: **March 22** The National Hockey League (NHL) and the World Hockey Association (WHA) merge.

1979: **May 21** The Montreal Canadiens win their third consecutive Stanley Cup hockey championship.

Overview

Two words described sports in the 1970s: big business. Owners and athletes in major professional team sports knew there was entertainment money to be made in their games, and they went after it. Owners and league officials sought additional revenue through mergers and expansions of their respective leagues. They also signed lucrative television contracts worth millions of dollars to bring their games into the homes of millions of Americans.

The sports entertainment business was highly competitive and only the strong survived—athletes as well as teams. Knowing this, athletes sought higher salaries. By the end of the decade, top athletes demanded, and were paid, over one million dollars a year to compete. Ironically, the athlete who started the fight for recognition and higher salaries—baseball player Curt Flood—not only never benefited, he eventually lost his career as a result of his actions.

Athletes in individual sports, such as golf and tennis, also saw their earnings rise in the 1970s. Yet again, for some, that money did not come without a fight. Neglected by the major team sports, women had to realize their athletic dreams in individual pursuits. But they were paid far less than their fellow male athletes, so they fought for equality. Leading the charge on the tennis courts was Billie Jean King. Her victory over Bobby Riggs paved the way not only for future female tennis players, but also for female athletes in other sports.

African American athletes were responsible for some of the decade's highest athletic achievements. Early in 1974, Hank Aaron surpassed Babe Ruth's career home run record, which had stood for thirty-nine years. Despite earning spectacular salaries, though, African American and other minority athletes lacked a voice in management. In 1974, Frank Robinson became baseball's first African American manager, but he was an exception. Few minorities held front office positions and none owned a team. Racial equality in positions of power in sports was still decades away.

Many believed sports should exist as a showcase of pure athletic competition, free of the affairs of politics and the outside world. The Olympic Games were founded on such an ideal. Yet the greed of team owners and professional athletes, and the tragic events in Munich on a September morning in 1972, proved that ideal was just an illusion—changing sports forever.

Muhammad Ali (1942–) Heavyweight boxing champion Muhammad Ali was the most publicized sports personality of the 1970s. Charismatic and articulate, he was a sensation both in and out of the ring. In a six-year period beginning in October 1970, Ali met twenty-two opponents, losing just two matches and winning more than $26 million in prize money. In 1974, in what is now simply referred to as "The Fight," Ali knocked out hard-hitting George Foreman to win the heavyweight crown, becoming only the second man ever to regain the title after having lost it. ***Photo reproduced by permission of Carl Nesfield.***

Billie Jean King (1943–) In 1971, Billie Jean King became the first woman to earn $100,000 as a professional tennis player. Since women champions on the professional tour were often awarded two to three times less prize money than their male counterparts, King began a vocal campaign to equalize the compensation. She soon succeeded. In 1973, in what may have been the most publicized event in American tennis history, King defeated Bobby Riggs in a match dubbed the "Battle of the Sexes." That same year, she helped establish the Women's Tennis Association, a union that lobbied for women's rights on the professional tour. ***Photo reproduced by permission of the Corbis Corporation.***

O.J. Simpson (1947–) Football star O. J. Simpson forged a new running style that would be emulated by the next generation of football players. A college standout, he was a national celebrity by the time the Buffalo Bills drafted him in 1969. During the 1970s, he led all running backs with 10,539 rushing yards, 25 percent more than second-place Franco Harris of the Pittsburgh Steelers. In 1978, Simpson became the highest paid professional football player when he signed a contract to play for the San Francisco 49ers for $806,668 per year. ***Photo reproduced by permission of the Corbis Corporation.***

Mark Spitz (1950–) Swimming sensation Mark Spitz was one of the most recognizable men in America in the 1970s as his Olympic achievements made him a celebrity. In 1971, the American Athletic Union named Spitz amateur athlete of the year. The following year, at the Olympic trials in August, he set a world record in the 200–meter butterfly. And in the 1972 Summer Olympics held shortly afterward in Munich, Germany, Spitz was stunning, winning seven gold medals. In every event in which he competed, four individual and three team events, he or his team set world records. ***Photo reproduced by permission of the Corbis Corporation.***

BASEBALL: FREE AGENCY, MONEY, AND GREED

At the beginning of the 1970s, baseball was struggling. Its innocence had been lost long ago, and now it faced disgrace. Public scandals, labor disputes, greed, and arrogance characterized the nation's game. It took more and more spectacular plays every year to draw the fans' attentions back to the field.

The relationship between players and owners, difficult since baseball's early days, became even more quarrelsome. Traditionally, professional athletes had been considered property whose value rested in a team owner or manager with the ability to market his players' skills. Players belonged to the teams that drafted them, and any player could be traded at the whim of an owner. In 1970, a lone player challenged baseball's reserve clause, which defined a player as property belonging to the team that holds his contract. It was a challenge that cost the player his career and changed the face of baseball forever.

When St. Louis Cardinals outfielder Curt Flood was traded to the Philadelphia Phillies against his will in late 1969, he balked and filed a lawsuit the following year against major league baseball over the reserve clause. Flood wanted the right to choose where and for whom he would play ball. Flood's lawyers argued that since professional baseball was controlled solely by the teams' owners, it was a monopoly. This meant that power and the concentration of wealth was in the hands of a select few, and normal marketplace or business competition was suppressed. Since baseball was a monopoly, the lawyers argued, it violated antitrust (antimonopoly) laws passed by the U.S. Congress in the late nineteenth century. In 1972, however, the U. S. Supreme Court ruled that its 1922 decision to exclude major league baseball from antitrust laws was still legal. Flood lost his case.

But Marvin Miller, executive director of the Major League Baseball Players' Association, had already begun a more effective means of toppling the hated reserve clause. Little by little, he chipped away at it, first crafting an agreement in 1973 between owners and players that allowed salary disputes to be settled through arbitration (judgment of a dispute by an impartial person or group). Then Miller convinced the owners to agree that any player who had ten years in the major leagues and five with the same team could veto a trade he did not like. Finally, in 1975, Miller found a loophole in the reserve clause. An arbitrator upheld the players' association's contention that if a player worked for a year without a contract, he could declare himself a free agent and market his services to the highest bidder. A year later, twenty-four players took advantage of the new ruling. As the American League added teams in Seattle and Toronto, twelve of the new free agents signed multiyear contracts for more than $1 million. Baseball had entered a new big-money era.

Greed marked the game in other ways as well. The Washington Senators, who had played in the nation's capital for eleven years, moved to Dallas in 1971, where they became the Texas Rangers. The possibility of making more money was the reason given for the move, underscoring the fact that baseball was (and is) purely business. In the latter part of the decade, the New York Yankees were good enough to win three straight pennants and two World Series. But they had a team payroll of $3.5 million, with eleven players earning over $100,000 a year. As critics claimed, they were the best team money could buy.

In spite of these excesses, there were moments of pure athletic achievement on the ball fields. In 1971, Oakland Athletics pitcher Vida Blue won his first ten games of the season, eventually finishing the year with twenty-four wins. In 1974, three veterans set new records: Atlanta Braves outfielder Hank Aaron broke Babe Ruth's career home-run record of 714; St. Louis Cardinals pitcher Bob Gibson struck out his three-thousandth batter; and Gibson's teammate, outfielder Lou Brock, stole a record 118 bases. In 1979, another veteran led his team to victory. Thirty-eight-year-old Willie Stargell, called "Pops" by his younger teammates, helped his Pittsburgh Pirates team overcome a three-games-to-one deficit to win the World Series. Stargell hit for a.400 batting average during the series, with a home run in the seventh game. He won every most-valuable-player award available.

BASKETBALL: RISING SALARIES AND FALLING ATTENDANCE

Like their baseball counterparts, professional basketball players saw their salaries rise dramatically in the 1970s. At the end of the 1960s, salaries for the players had averaged $43,000 a season. Just ten years later, 240 professional basketball players averaged $158,000 a year in salaries, an increase of over 250 percent. The league itself was in similarly great financial shape, having signed a lucrative television contract with CBS in 1972. On average, each team in the National Basketball Association (NBA) received about $800,000 a year in revenue from the TV contract.

But fan interest did not match the high salaries and wide television coverage. Indeed, television ratings slipped badly by the end of the decade. Game attendance also fell, brought about, in part, by relatively high-ticket prices around the league. Although critics pointed out many reasons for dwindling fan interest, some people believed the main reason was racism: As the number of African American players increased during

World Series Champions

Year	Winning Team/Games Won	Losing Team/Games Won
1970	Baltimore Orioles (AL) 4	Cincinnati Reds (NL) 1
1971	Pittsburgh Pirates (NL) 4	Baltimore Orioles (AL) 3
1972	Oakland Athletics (AL) 4	Cincinnati Reds (NL) 3
1973	Oakland Athletics (AL) 4	New York Mets (NL) 3
1974	Oakland Athletics (AL) 4	Los Angeles Dodgers (NL) 1
1975	Cincinnati Reds (NL) 4	Boston Red Sox (AL) 3
1976	Cincinnati Reds (NL) 4	New York Yankees (AL) 0
1977	New York Yankees (AL) 4	Los Angeles Dodgers (NL) 2
1978	New York Yankees (AL) 4	Los Angeles Dodgers (NL) 2
1979	Pittsburgh Pirates (NL) 4	Baltimore Orioles (AL) 3

the decade (making up 75 percent of all players by the end of the 1970s), the interest of white fans decreased.

Most critics, however, blamed the lack of fan interest on the lack of a team concept within the NBA. They felt that team owners were more interested in showcasing individual superstars who could put on a show than in team play that could win a championship. A street-ball style of play had come to dominate the NBA during the decade, with an emphasis placed on a player's offensive flair within the key (area under and in front of the basket) and his ability to dunk. Perhaps no player best epitomized that flair than Julius Erving.

Known as "Doctor J," Erving had been drafted by the Virginia Squires of the American Basketball Association (ABA) in 1971. The ABA existed as a competing league to the NBA from 1967 to 1976. With its red, white, and blue ball and three-point field goal, the ABA was flashier than the NBA, but after just nine seasons, it found it could not compete with the financially secure older league. When the ABA folded in 1976, four of its teams and many of its players moved to the NBA. Among those players was the ABA's biggest star, Doctor J.

Erving's ability to defy gravity left audiences shaking their heads in disbelief. His dunks and delicate finger-roll shots often started with a leap from

Defying gravity, Julius "Doctor J" Erving goes up for a basket. **Reproduced by permission of AP/Wide World Photos.**

NBA Champions

Year	Winning Team/Games Won	Losing Team/Games Won
1970	New York Knicks 4	Los Angeles Lakers 3
1971	Milwaukee Bucks 4	Baltimore Bullets 0
1972	Los Angeles Lakers 4	New York Knicks 1
1973	New York Knicks 4	Los Angeles Lakers 1
1974	Boston Celtics 4	Milwaukee Bucks 3
1975	Golden State Warriors 4	Washington Bullets 0
1976	Boston Celtics 4	Phoenix Suns 2
1977	Portland Trail Blazers 4	Philadelphia 76ers 2
1978	Washington Bullets 4	Seattle SuperSonics 3
1979	Seattle SuperSonics 4	Washington Bullets 1

the foul line. After the merger of the two leagues, Erving moved on to the Philadelphia 76ers, becoming part of one of the most talented teams of the 1970s. Considered the most gifted pro basketball player of his generation, Erving combined grace, strength, court presence, and imagination. He created a new style of offensive play that would be copied by other guards and small forwards, and later further refined by Michael Jordan of the Chicago Bulls.

With the birth of the era of the superstar in the NBA, few teams dominated play in the 1970s. Early in the decade, the league's most popular team was the New York Knicks. Willis Reed, Bill Bradley, Dave DeBusschere, Dick Barnett, and Walt Frazier formed the core of a team that blended like no other. Their play was often inspirational. But even the Knicks failed to create a dynasty, winning only two nonconsecutive NBA titles during the decade. The only other team to match that feat in the 1970s was the once powerful Boston Celtics. With no domineering team to love or hate, basketball fans sat quietly in their seats or simply left the arenas. It would take the superstars of the next decade to bring them back.

FOOTBALL: AMERICA'S GAME AND AMERICA'S TEAM

Unlike baseball or basketball, professional football did not have a problem keeping fans in their seats during the 1970s. Indeed, football had

Super Bowl Champions

Year	Winning Team/Score	Losing Team/Score
1970	Kansas City 23	Minnesota 7
1971	Baltimore Colts 16	Dallas Cowboys 13
1972	Dallas Cowboys 24	Miami Dolphins 3
1973	Miami Dolphins 14	Washington Redskins 7
1974	Miami Dolphins 24	Minnesota Vikings 7
1975	Pittsburgh Steelers 16	Minnesota Vikings 6
1976	Pittsburgh Steelers 21	Dallas Cowboys 17
1977	Oakland Raiders 32	Minnesota Vikings 14
1978	Dallas Cowboys 27	Denver Broncos 10
1979	Pittsburgh Steelers 35	Dallas Cowboys 31

become America's game by the end of the decade. A 1978 Harris sports survey showed that football enjoyed a 70 percent following among American sports fans, compared to only 54 percent for baseball. Record numbers of American families viewed Super Bowls VI through XIV on their televisions, making the glitzy, heavily hyped championship between the American and National Football Conferences one of the most-watched sporting events of all time.

In 1970, football became a big hit in prime-time television because of ABC's *Monday Night Football.* Throughout the rest of the 1970s, on Sunday afternoons and Monday evenings during the season, in family living rooms and local bars, it seemed as if all of America were watching professional football.

Enormous change in the sport took place at the beginning of the decade. The merger between the National Football League (NFL; formed in 1922) and the American Football League (AFL; formed in 1960) was finalized for the 1970 season, four years after the two leagues had reached an agreement. The new league, called the National Football League, was composed of two new conferences: Three former NFL teams—the Baltimore Colts, the Cleveland Browns, and the Pittsburgh Steelers—joined with former AFL clubs to create the American Football Conference; the rest of the old NFL teams became the National Football Conference.

Former AFL teams brought much to the stale NFL, including an innovative brand of offensive and defensive football. In the early 1970s, one of those former AFL teams, the Miami Dolphins, began a dynasty that many fans and sportswriters thought would rule over the pro ranks for a decade. They made three straight appearances in the Super Bowl—1971, 1972, and 1973—winning the championship in their last two trips. In 1972, they became the only NFL team ever to post a perfect season record. The Dolphins won all 14 of their regular-season games, two playoffs games, and Super Bowl VII to finish with a 17–0 record.

The next team to assume the mantle as the NFL's best was the Pittsburgh Steelers. For nearly four previous decades, the Steelers had labored at or near the bottom of the pro standings. But with a new crop of talented players such as Terry Bradshaw, Mean Joe Green, L. C. Greenwood, Lynn Swann, and Franco Harris, the Steelers made four Super Bowl appearances—1974, 1975, 1978, and 1979—winning every time. In the 1972 AFC divisional play-off game between Pittsburgh and the Oakland Raiders, with 22 seconds left on the clock, Bradshaw passed the ball to running

Franco Harris (number 32) of the Pittsburgh Steelers eludes tackler Jimmy Ware of the Oakland Raiders in what became known as the "Immaculate Reception." **Reproduced by permission of AP/Wide World Photos.**

back John ("Frenchy") Fuqua, who collided with Raiders safety Jack Tatum. The ball ricocheted off one of the two into the hands of Harris, who in full sprint caught the ball and ran in to the end zone for what officials later decided was the winning touchdown. Despite the continuing controversy over who touched the ball first, the "Immaculate Reception," as it is now known, remains one of the most memorable plays in football history.

The Steelers' dominance was unquestioned, but another team actually made more trips to the Super Bowl during the decade. The Dallas Cowboys played in the championship game five times. Under head coach Tom Landry, the Cowboys were perhaps pro football's most consistent team. Although they won the Super Bowl only twice, in 1971 and 1977, fans across the country rightly expected them to win the big games. By the end of the 1970s, Dallas had become known as America's team.

HOCKEY: A BULLYING ERA

Mergers, shrinking attendance, and rising salaries, characteristics that came to define both professional baseball and professional basketball in the 1970s, also marked professional hockey. Knowing theirs was a business like all other professional sports, National Hockey League (NHL) owners and officials sought to maximize the amount of money the league made. They increased the number of teams in the league, expanding into markets without hockey traditions such as Los Angeles, Atlanta, and Kansas City. By 1975, the league had grown to eighteen teams, triple the number of teams only a decade before. The expansion left many sportswriters and longtime hockey fans fearing that the quality of play would diminish. Indeed, with each added team, talent became spread more thinly across the league.

The NHL also lost talented players to the World Hockey Association (WHA), formed in 1971 by two California entrepreneurs. In 1972, the WHA landed its first superstar when the Winnipeg Jets paid superstar Bobby Hull of the Chicago Blackhawks a $1-million bonus to sign a ten-year contract worth $2.75 million. Hull's contract marked the beginning of bidding wars between the two leagues.

As players' salaries rose, severe financial hardships were felt by many teams in both the NHL and WHA. As early as 1973, secret talks were held to discuss a merger between the two leagues. A deal was not reached until 1979, when the WHA agreed to disband. Four former WHA franchises—the Edmonton Oilers, the Hartford Whalers, the Quebec Nordiques, and the Winnipeg Jets—joined the NHL, bringing the number of teams in the league to twenty-one.

Stanley Cup Champions

Year	Winning Team/Games Won	Losing Team/Games Won
1970	Boston Bruins 4	St. Louis Blues 0
1971	Montreal Canadiens 4	Chicago Blackhawks 3
1972	Boston Bruins 4	New York Rangers 2
1973	Montreal Canadiens 4	Chicago Blackhawks 2
1974	Philadelphia Flyers 4	Boston Bruins 2
1975	Philadelphia Flyers 4	Buffalo Sabres 2
1976	Montreal Canadiens 4	Philadelphia Flyers 0
1977	Montreal Canadiens 4	Boston Bruins 0
1978	Montreal Canadiens 4	Boston Bruins 2
1979	Montreal Canadiens 4	New York Rangers 1

The face of hockey changed in other ways during the 1970s. It became a less graceful, meaner sport. Early in the decade, the Boston Bruins, led by Phil Esposito and Bobby Orr, introduced a rugged, blue-collar style of play that emphasized hard checking and slap shots. Their swagger and talent helped them win the Stanley Cup in 1970 and 1972 and reach the finals in 1974.

The "Big Bad Bruins," however, soon were replaced by the Philadelphia Flyers, also known as the Broad Street Bullies. With their bloody-knuckled style of play, they quickly became the nightmare of most NHL players. On the ice, the Flyers were charged with an astounding number of penalty minutes. During the 1974–75 season, enforcer Dave ("The Hammer") Schultz earned a record 472 minutes alone. But the Flyers' reign over the NHL was not based solely on their fists. They could score goals, too. Led by captain Bobby Clarke, a brilliant passer and one of the finest centers in the league, the Flyers captured the Stanley Cup in 1974 and 1975.

Just when many would-be fans were writing off hockey as a brawling spectacle, the Montreal Canadiens returned class to the NHL. Emphasizing speed and the brilliant offensive play of Guy Lafleur, Montreal won the Stanley Cup four straight times, beginning in 1976. Soon other teams were trading and drafting for speed rather than size. In 1979, when the

Edmonton Oilers joined the NHL following the merger, the team featured a teenage phenomenon named Wayne Gretzky. Many thought he was too small to compete, but that season he scored fifty-one goals and had eighty six assists. In doing so, he ushered in a new era of hockey.

GOLF: THE GAME OPENS UP AND A LEGEND APPEARS

Prior to the 1970s, many Americans viewed golf as a snobbish game played by the rich. As the decade progressed, that view quickly changed. In 1971, as millions of Americans watched on television, *Apollo 14* astronaut Alan B. Shepard sent a six-iron shot sailing in the Moon's thin atmosphere. His enthusiasm for golf soon spread throughout middle-class America. With the development of more and more public golf courses, millions of Americans headed out to the links with mass-produced clubs and balls. Expanded television coverage of men's Professional Golf Association (PGA) Tour events also helped bring greater attention to the game during the decade.

Lee Treviño was one of the most talented golfers of the 1970s. **Reproduced by permission of the Corbis Corporation.**

Partly responsible for increasing golf's popularity with Americans was golfer Arnold Palmer. In the 1960s, Palmer was seen as an everyman on the golf course, and legions of fans copied his swashbuckling, go-for-broke style. While amateur players filled the public courses, trying to emulate their new hero Palmer, a long-hitting Ohioan named Jack Nicklaus began challenging Palmer's rule. By the 1970s, Nicklaus seemed to be winning every tournament in sight and had claimed all four major golf titles: the Masters, the PGA Tournament, the U.S. Open, and the British Open. Nicklaus was Palmer's successor, but as the decade progressed, many became convinced that Nicklaus had surpassed all of his predecessors to become golf's greatest player ever.

Nicklaus ruled over the golf world in the 1970s. Throughout the decade, talented players such as Lee Treviño, Tom Weiskopf, Ben Crenshaw, Tom Kite, and Johnny Miller challenged his position. In 1974, Miller had one of professional golf's greatest years, winning eight tournaments. Within a few years, however, Miller began to fade, and Nicklaus remained on top. In 1975, Nicklaus won a fifth Masters tournament, and in 1978 he

PGA Player of the Year

Year	Player
1970	Billy Casper
1971	Lee Treviño
1972	Jack Nicklaus
1973	Jack Nicklaus
1974	Johnny Miller
1975	Jack Nicklaus
1976	Jack Nicklaus
1977	Tom Watson
1978	Tom Watson
1979	Tom Watson

won another British Open, giving him at least three victories in all four major tournaments. Only one player, Tom Watson, successfully unseated Nicklaus as golf's best, albeit for a short time. From 1977 to 1979, Watson was the only golfer who outplayed Nicklaus, and he earned three straight Player of the Year honors for his achievements.

Although the golf world opened up in the 1970s, it did so slowly for minorities and women. Robert Lee Elder was the only prominent African American on the professional tour. He captured his first PGA title in 1974 at the Monsanto Open. Elder won twice in 1978, then in 1979 he became the first African American to play for America's Ryder Cup team (the Ryder Cup tournament is a biennial match between teams of players from the United States and Europe).

In women's golf, fewer events, fewer corporate sponsors, and less television coverage meant less money and recognition for players on the Ladies Professional Golf Association (LPGA) Tour. What the tour did not lack, however, was talent. In 1978, junior golfing sensation Nancy Lopez burst onto the LPGA Tour and became what women's golf needed most: a star. She dominated the tour that year with nine victories, including five consecutive wins, stunning the sports world. She took Player of the Year honors as well as Rookie of the Year, a feat no one had accomplished before. She repeated as Player of the Year in 1979, having won eight more tournaments. Lopez's dominating presence on the golf course further revolutionized women's golf during the next decade, as purses became richer and fans and the media began to pay greater attention to the LPGA Tour.

TENNIS: THE GAME TO PLAY

While football became America's sport to watch during the 1970s, tennis became America's game to play. Tennis became the "in" sport. The country's middle class embraced tennis, spending millions of dollars on equipment and clothing. By the end of the decade, it was estimated that more than a quarter of America's population—and a nearly equal number of blacks and whites—played tennis at least four times a year.

Tennis in the United States became a whirlwind of change. Television-friendly yellow balls replaced white ones; splashy colors became a part of tennis fashion; metal and graphite replaced wood in rackets built to be stronger, larger, and more powerful; and tournament prize money for the winners jumped from the thousands to the hundreds of thousands of dollars.

Two televised matches in the early 1970s were largely responsible for this tennis boom. In 1972, Rod Laver and Ken Rosewall, two legendary Australian players, met in Dallas for the World Championship Tennis (WCT) finals. The three-hour-and-forty-five-minute tennis marathon, shown on CBS, glued viewers to their televisions. The network even preempted its regular evening shows in order to broadcast the entire match.

The second televised match, held in the fall of 1973, was the much-publicized "Battle of the Sexes" between Billie Jean King and Bobby Riggs. King not only won the lopsided match against the fifty-five-year-old Riggs, but she also won the goodwill of the American public. King went on to use her publicity to fight for and win more prize money and better conditions for her fellow women tennis players.

Outstanding achievements marked both the men's and the women's professional tour. In 1975, Arthur Ashe became the first African American to win the famed Wimbledon men's singles championship, defeating fellow American Jimmy Connors. This defeat did little to dim Connors's star as he and Chris Evert ruled as the king and queen of American tennis. They brought youth, brash attitude, and even a little romance to the game.

Engaged at one time to be married, Connors and Evert each became Wimbledon singles champions in 1974. Two years later, in only her third year on the tour, Evert became the first woman to earn $1 million in prize money. She simply dominated the other women, winning twelve of seven-

U.S. Open Tennis Tournament Champions

Year	Male	Female
1970	Ken Rosewall	Margaret Smith Court
1971	Stan Smith	Billie Jean King
1972	Ilie Nastase	Billie Jean King
1973	John Newcombe	Margaret Smith Court
1974	Jimmy Connors	Billie Jean King
1975	Manuel Orantes	Chris Evert
1976	Jimmy Connors	Chris Evert
1977	Guillermo Vilas	Chris Evert
1978	Jimmy Connors	Chris Evert
1979	John McEnroe	Tracy Austin

teen tournaments that year. High-school students everywhere emulated her baseline style punctuated by her two-handed backhand.

Connors was a new breed of player. His two-handed backhand, metal racket, and arrogant attitude challenged tennis convention. He was subject to temper tantrums on the court, but his fiery brand of competition endeared him to many fans. By decade's end, though, many began to question developments in the game, as the tantrums of Connors and his American successor John McEnroe were being adopted by players in junior tennis events across the nation. Critics warned that the game was becoming too fast-paced, too rich, and too obnoxious.

❖ THE OLYMPICS: GLORY AND TRAGEDY

The 1972 Winter Olympics, held in Sapporo, Japan, featured 800 male and 206 female athletes from thirty-five nations. Athletes from the United States won a total of eight medals, including three gold medals—all won by women. Skier Barbara Cochran took gold in the slalom, while two other American women won gold medals in speed skating; sixteen-year-old world-record-holder Anne Henning won the 500-meter competition, and Dianne Holum won the 1500 meters. Holum also won a speed-skating silver in the 3000 meters.

American Cathy Rigby performs during the compulsory gymnastic team competition at the 1972 Munich Olympics. That year, the Los Angeles Times *named her Sportswoman of the Year.* **Reproduced by permission of AP/Wide World Photos.**

The summer games that year were held in Munich in the former West Germany, drawing a record number of nations and athletes. From 121 nations, 6,065 men and 1,058 women competed. Although American athletes won ninety-three medals, thirty-three of them gold, only the swimmers performed according to expectations. And they were magnificent, dominating the competition. The men's and women's team each won nine gold medals, setting a total of twelve world records in the process. The star of the pool was Mark Spitz, who won seven gold medals in four individual and three team events. In each of those events, he or his team set a world record.

The defining moment of the summer games, however, was tragic. On the morning of September 5, eight Arab members of the organization

American figure skater Dorothy Hamill became a national sensation after winning the gold medal during the 1976 Winter Olympics. **Reproduced by permission of Archive Photos, Inc.**

Black September broke into the Israeli compound, murdered two athletes, and kidnapped nine others. The terrorists demanded the release of two hundred Arab guerrilla fighters held in Israeli prisons. When the terrorists and their hostages made their way to the Munich airport, an Israeli antiterrorist team tried to rescue the athletes. Five of the terrorists and all nine of the hostages were killed in the encounter. The games were suspended for thirty-four hours, and a memorial for the slain athletes was held in the main stadium.

Four years later, the 1976 Winter Olympics were held in Innsbruck, Austria, with 892 male and 231 female athletes from thirty-seven countries competing. For Americans, all of the winning opportunities came on the ice. Dorothy Hamill upset reigning world champion Dianne de Leeuw to win the gold medal in women's figure skating. Speed skater Peter Mueller won gold in the 1000 meters, and fellow skater Sheila Young won gold in the 500 meters, setting an Olympic record. Young, who also won a silver in the 1500 meters and a bronze in the 1000 meters, accounted for nearly a third of the ten medals won by American athletes.

Political controversy, a hallmark of the Olympic Games since World War II (1939–45), surrounded the 1976 Summer Olympics held in Montreal, Canada. By the time the games began, thirty-two nations had for various reasons declared a boycott. Ninety-two nations sent teams composed of 4,781 male and 1,247 female athletes. Once again, the United States finished second to the former Soviet Union in the total medals category, winning 94 medals (34 gold) to the Soviets' 125 medals (47 gold). Outstanding achievements by American athletes included Bruce Jenner winning gold in the decathlon and swimmer John Nabor winning four gold medals, setting two world records along the way. Sugar Ray Leonard and brothers Michael and Leon Spinks claimed three of the five gold medals won by American boxers. All three would go on to dominate professional boxing in the 1980s.

For More Information

BOOKS

Miller, Marvin. *A Whole Different Ballgame: The Sport and Business of Baseball.* Secaucus, NJ: Carol Publishing Group, 1991.

Myers, Walter Dean. *The Greatest: Muhammad Ali.* New York: Scholastic, 2001.

Nicklaus, Jack, and Ken Bowden. *Jack Nicklaus: My Story.* New York: Simon and Schuster, 1997.

Pluto, Terry. *Loose Balls: The Short, Wild Life of the American Basketball Association.* New York: Fireside, 1991.

Reeve, Simon. *One Day in September: The Full Story of the 1972 Munich Olympics Massacre and the Israeli Revenge Operation.* New York: Arcade Publishing, 2000.

WEB SITES

Miller, Marvin. *A Whole Different Ballgame: The Sport and Business of Baseball.* Secaucus, NJ: Carol Publishing Group, 1991.

Julius Erving [Online] http://www.hoophall.com/halloffamers/Erving.htm (accessed on February 27, 2002).

1970s Flashback: 70s Sports News. [Online] http://www.1970sflashback.com/1970/Sports.asp (accessed on February 27, 2002).

Wide World of Sports Highlights: 1970s. [Online] http://espn.go.com/abcsports/wwos/milestones/1970s.html (accessed on February 27, 2002).

Where to Learn More

BOOKS

Braunstein, Peter, and Michael William Doyle, eds. *Imagine Nation: The American Counterculture of the 1960s and '70s*. New York: Routledge, 2001.

Carroll, Peter N. *It Seemed Like Nothing Happened: America in the 1970s*. Reprint ed. Piscataway, NJ: Rutgers University Press, 1990.

Edelstein, Andrew J., and Kevin McDonough. *The Seventies: From Hot Pants to Hot Tubs*. New York: Dutton, 1990.

Frum, David. *How We Got Here: The 70's, The Decade that Brought You Modern Life-For Better or Worse*. New York: Basic Books, 2000.

Matthews, Scott. *Stuck in the Seventies: 113 Things from the 1970s that Screwed Up the Twentysomething Generation*. Chicago, IL: Bonus Books, 1995.

Schmidt, Mark Ray, ed. *The 1970s*. San Diego, CA: Greenhaven Press, 2000.

Schulman, Bruce J. *The Seventies: The Great Shift in American Culture, Society, and Politics*. New York: Free Press, 2001.

Stewart, Gail B., ed. *The 1970s*. San Diego, CA: Lucent, 1999.

Time-Life Books, ed. *Time of Transition: The 70s*. Alexandria, VA: Time-Life Books, 1998.

Waldrep, Shelton. *The Seventies: The Age of Glitter in Popular Culture*. New York: Routledge, 1999.

WEB SITES

American Cultural History. http://www.nhmccd.cc.tx.us/contracts/lrc/kc/decade70.html (accessed on June 1, 2002).

Where to Learn More

Biography of America: Contemporary History. http://www.learner.org/biographyof america/prog25/index.html (accessed on June 1, 2002).

1860–2000 General History: 1970s. http://cdcga.org/HTMLs/decades/1970s.htm (accessed on June 1, 2002).

Greatest Space Events of the 20th Century. http://www.space.com/news/space history/greatest_70s_991230.html (accessed on June 1, 2002).

History Channel. http://www.historychannel.com/index.html (accessed on June 1, 2002).

Map: Political Systems on the World in the 1970s. http://users.erols.com/ mwhite28/govt1970.htm (accessed on June 1, 2002).

Media History Timeline: 1970s. http://www.mediahistory.umn.edu/time/1970s. html (accessed on June 1, 2002).

1970s Flashback: 1970–1979. http://www.1970sflashback.com/ (accessed on June 1, 2002).

Nobel e-Museum. http://www.nobel.se/ (accessed June 1, 2002).

Official Website of the Olympic Movement. http://www.olympic.org/uk/index_uk. asp (accessed on June 1, 2002).

Super 70s.com. http://www.super70s.com/Super70s/ (accessed on June 1, 2002).

20th Century American Culture. http://members.aol.com/TeacherNet/20CC.html (accessed on June 1, 2002).

20th Century Decades: 1970–1979 Decade. http://dewey.chs.chico.k12.ca.us/ decs7.html (accessed on June 1, 2002).

20th Century Fashion History: 1970s. http://www.costumegallery.com/1970.htm (accessed on June 1, 2002).

20th Century History. http://history1900s.about.com/ (accessed on June 1, 2002).

Index

C

D

E

F

I

J

K

L

P

U

V

Z